Dialogue, Catalogue & Monologue

Personal, Impersonal and Depersonalizing
Ways to Use Words

Dialogue, Catalogue & Monologue

Personal, Impersonal and Depersonalizing Ways to Use Words

Craig M. Gay

R

Regent College Publishing

www.regentpublishing.com

For my parents

Published 2008 by Regent College Publishing
5800 University Boulevard, Vancouver, BC V6T 2E4 Canada
Web: www.regentpublishing.com
E-mail: info@regentpublishing.com

Regent College Publishing is an imprint of the Regent College Bookstore
<www.regentbookstore.com>. Views expressed in works published by Regent
College Publishing are those of the author and do not necessarily represent
the official position of Regent College <www.regent-college.edu>.

Book design by Robert Hand
<roberthandcommunications.com>

Biblical citations are taken from *The New International Version* (NIV).

ISBN 10: 1-57383-374-6
ISBN 13: 9-781-57383-374-5

Library and Archives Canada Cataloguing in Publication

Gay, Craig M.
Dialogue, catalogue & monologue: personal, impersonal and
depersonalizing ways to use words / Craig M. Gay.

Includes bibliographical references.

1. Dialogue—Religious aspects—Christianity. 2. Interpersonal
communication—Religious aspects—Christianity. 3. Word of God
(Theology). 4. Miscommunication. I. Title. II. Title: Dialogue,
catalogue and monologue.

P94.7.G39 2008   248   C2008-900014-5

Contents

Acknowledgments

THERE ARE A NUMBER of people I would like to thank for helping me to research and write this short book. Two of my teaching assistants at Regent College, Carol McMahan and Christian Amondson, helped to investigate several of the specific topics discussed in the following chapters. Another teaching assistant, Paul Martens, introduced me to the work of Nelly Viallaneix whose elucidation of Søren Kierkegaard's "theology of listening" figures prominently in chapter 4. Paul's English translations of several of Viallaneix's articles are also quite a bit better than any I could have produced. In addition, my friends and colleagues Jim Houston, Maxine Hancock and Steven Kent offered to read an early draft of the book and made helpful suggestions for revising it. I am also grateful for the first-rate editorial talents of Karen Wuest and Kathy Tyers and for the patience of Regent College Publishing's Bill Reimer and Rob Clements. Finally, I want to express my deepest gratitude to my wife, Julie, and to our four children. A great deal of what I have learned about the healing power of words I have learned from them.

Prologue

THIS BOOK IS ABOUT words and the attitudes that we take toward them. Its purpose is simply to encourage us to take the words that we speak more seriously than we are perhaps in the habit of doing. The contemporary situation is such that we have become used to the deceptive subtleties and half-truths that characterize so many of the words that reach our eyes and ears. This is perhaps most obvious in the political arena, where we expect the words of politicians to be spun to specific political purposes; but political figures are not the only ones who have formed the habit of using words mendaciously and manipulatively. Indeed, our political representatives are only applying techniques long since developed by preachers, advertisers, media producers, lawyers, university professors, and others who would seek to sway us in various directions and whose primary tools for doing so are words.

We are also surrounded by many foolish words that fail to shed light on our circumstances. Many of these words combine to form "chatter," empty words not really intended to communicate anything at all but spoken either to titillate and entertain or simply to fill what vacant time and space there may happen to be. Other words purport to be veracious but aren't. Of the thousands of words that we see and hear each day having to do with sex and sexuality, for example, how many of them actually shed any light on either? Of the words that purport to tell us where personal fulfillment is to be found, how many actually do? Of all of the talk about religion and spirituality today, how much of it is actually edifying? Such chatter is not always deceitful—it is often well intended and sincere—but it fails to disclose the truth of things. These foolish words are, like the advice of Job's friends, "without knowledge," obscuring and not illuminating our situations.

We have also been hurt by words, especially words spoken by those closest to us, and we have used words to hurt those we love in turn. An old adage has it that "the knives of saying cut the deepest,"[1] and they do indeed. The more familiar childhood apothegm—"Sticks and stones can break my bones, but words can never hurt me"—has it exactly wrong. In fact words can hurt us very, very deeply, just as they undoubtedly did when we last made use of this foolish quip. Words can obscure the truth of things. They can drive us away from each other, and they can prevent us from knowing and becoming ourselves. Indeed, words can crush our spirits more efficiently and effectively than perhaps any other single agency.

There are a great many reasons, then, why we have probably been tempted to abandon our faith in words and to back away from the words of others. We may even have been tempted to break faith with our own words and to step back away from the words that we speak. The central contention of this book, however, is that to back away from the words of others and to refrain from standing behind our own words is to back away from life itself. Words are at the essence of our existence, and the quality of the words we hear and speak all but determines the quality of our lives. Indeed, the One who said that heaven and earth would pass away but that his words would not also said, "I tell you that [you] will have to give account on the day of judgment for every careless word [you] have spoken. For by your words you will be acquitted, and by your words you will be condemned" (Mt 12:36–37).

If we are to be acquitted or condemned on the basis of our words, this is only because we are to be judged as responsible *human* persons, and responsible human existence hinges to a very large degree on the words that we speak. Unlike other animals, we do not find ourselves mortised into an environment by means of an instinctual apparatus, instinctively knowing and learning only what is immediately necessary for survival. Instead we find ourselves beholding our circumstances, as it were, at a distance, and desiring to know and to learn far more about the world than simple survival requires. We want to know *where* we are, *what* we are in relation to other creatures, *why* we are here, and *who* we are. These questions can only be answered in words. Consider the importance of the words that we call *names*. Naming fixes a distance between us and the things that we name, transforming the immediacy of simple awareness into thoughtfulness and consciousness. Naming begins to situate us in a meaningful *world*. Other words enable us to complete this world, words that enable us to tell others about the things that we have named, as well as about ourselves and our intentions. Naming, in short, is for the sake of telling, and both exist for the sake of intelligent discourse.[2] Such discourse is what makes the uniquely human form of life possible; that is, a life of communion based upon *verbal* communication. While other species appear to be wonderfully adapted to convey important information to one another by means of a variety of signs and signals, we are the only animals who speak, who construct a common world on the basis of words that we intentionally bestow upon our experience.

Our capacity for intelligent discourse thus enables us to transcend animal existence as such and to enter into the realm of *spirit*. For it is through our words—and particularly through the little word *I*—that we establish ourselves as freely acting subjects. We say I, furthermore, always and only in recognition of a *you*, a you who also recognizes us and says *I* and *you* back to us, perhaps even calling us by name. This mutual reciprocation in words and speech—*I* speaking to *you*, *you* answering *me*—enables us to become ourselves. It establishes us as *persons*. When *I* and *you* are combined with verbs like "promise," "declare," "love," and "believe," we perform *spirited* and profoundly significant actions in the world. And our shared commitment to such words enables us to say *We*.

Our lives, in short, consist in the reciprocating movement away from and toward the world and others—of distancing and relating—and both occur principally by means of words and speech.[3] The consciousness of self, after all, is the awareness that we stand at some distance from the world and from others and that we possess real freedom with respect to both. Words create this space. Yet to live is to move to bridge this distance, to choose to enter into relation with the world and with others, ideally in such a way that both are thereby liberated to be what they truly are over and against us. Words create this relation. Our words enable the relation of love.

But enough said. I will reiterate and develop these thoughts in the following chapters. My concern at the outset is simply to stress the profound significance of the words we speak and to suggest that to back away from them—as I believe we are sorely tempted to do these days—is to back away from the genuinely human form of life. It is as if having found that the well is poisoned, we have decided to try to live without water. But we cannot live without water, and neither can we live without words.

Dialogue, Catalogue, and Monologue

In the following study the words *dialogue, catalogue,* and *monologue* will stand for three distinct postures that it is possible for us to take with respect to our words. *Dialogue* will designate a posture of genuine conversation. We assume a posture of dialogue when we respect the words of others because they are spoken by persons intrinsically worthy of our respect. Dialogue requires us to take care with respect to the words we speak, standing behind them and owning up to them, so that we will not derail our conversation by misrepresenting ourselves to those with whom we converse. Dialogue is thus personalizing speech. It is, I will contend, what words and speech are primarily for. The term *monologue,* by contrast, will be used to denote a posture of willfulness. In a monologue there is only one speaker and one active voice, and words are employed simply as means to ends. Very often, the desired end is control. As the use of words as means to ends tends to be inimical to conversation, I will characterize monologue as depersonalizing speech. The word *catalogue,* finally, will stand for impersonal speech, the kind of speech that arises out of a posture of uncommitted observation. The posture of catalogue, in effect, collects words, knowledge, and information. Its aim is to produce a dictionary or, better, an encyclopedia containing all possible knowledge and know-how. Though not necessarily willful, catalogue remains ambivalent with respect to personal existence. Its desire is to accumulate knowledge but not necessarily to cultivate communion. Words spoken out of the posture of catalogue could, in principle, be spoken by anyone, to anyone else, and at any time.

Using these three words, *dialogue, catalogue,* and *monologue,* I want to advance a three-part argument: first, that dialogue— which is to say conversation for the sake of communion— though remaining the primary purpose of words and speech, has been all but overwhelmed in modern times by the aridity and impersonality of the language of catalogue. To put this in terms introduced earlier, a kind of abstract and technical naming has been allowed to overwhelm telling in modern times.[4] Furthermore, as the language of catalogue has been allowed to eclipse that of dialogue, social space has opened up for the insurgency of monologue—that is, for the increasingly willful and manipulative use of words and speech. As we have grown increasingly used to equivocation, sophistry, and other kinds of manipulative speech, however, we have become increasingly incapable of listening to each other and—what is infinitely more significant—*of listening for the voice of God.* The third part of my argument, then, will be to contend that we must resist this development, that we must somehow pull the posture of dialogue back out from beneath the burden of catalogue and monologue. Speaking and listening out of the posture of dialogue is requisite for fellowship, and fellowship— with each other and with God—is the deepest desire of our hearts. As Martin Buber observes:

> In our age, in which the true meaning of every word is encompassed by delusion and falsehood, and the original intention of the human glance is stifled by tenacious mistrust, it is of decisive importance to find again the genuineness of speech and existence as We. This is no longer a matter which concerns the small circles that have been so important in the essential history of man; this is a matter of leavening the human race in all places with genuine We-ness.[5]

If we are to find this genuineness of speech and existence as We, I believe we will need to try to understand just how and why, in modern times, dialogue has been concealed first beneath catalogue and subsequently beneath monologue. A good deal of what follows will be taken up in analyzing these developments. Among other things, this will help us to understand just how it is that our culture can be so full of words, knowledge, and information and yet at the same time so apparently empty of wisdom. Understanding how and why dialogue has been eclipsed within contemporary culture may also help us to understand the stubbornly secular quality of so much of contemporary culture. For true religion is a matter of hearing and then responding with deeply personal words, the significance of which is largely invisible to the objective bias of catalogue and hateful to the manipulative bent of monologue. Lastly, I believe that understanding the relations between dialogue, catalogue, and monologue sheds considerable light on the impersonal quality of so much of our culture and suggests that the defense of personal existence today must be marshaled, in large part, out of our cultivation of genuine dialogue. This is why, in spite of the time I devote to analysis in the following chapters, the thrust of this study is primarily ethical. I believe there is an intimate connection between the words that we speak and our neighbor's well-being, and that the attitude we take to our words has everything to do with who we are and who we will ultimately become. Owning up to our words, then, before each other and before God is a primary ethical task.

Admittedly, there are problems associated with trying to make the kind of case I have just outlined. The mysterious power of speech as well as the nature of the relations between our words and the world are notoriously difficult to put into words. As St. Augustine observed: the "treating of words by means of words is as complicated a business as interlocking and rubbing the fingers of one hand with the fingers of the other, where it is scarcely discernible, except by the one doing it, which fingers are itching and which are relieving the itch."[6] Analyzing the contemporary abuse of language along the lines I have indicated also runs the risk of objectifying the problem and thus contributing to the kind of pseudo-knowledge that, as Kierkegaard might have contended, leaves a person's "inwardness" completely unmoved. After all, being able to locate the contemporary abuse of language in the history of ideas and mustering the courage to own up to our own words are two entirely different matters.

And, of course, the whole project may seem hopelessly naive. Haven't Nietzsche, Marx, Freud and other modern "masters of suspicion" shown that words are never what they seem to be, that they always mask subconscious drives or vested interests, that words simply float like froth on the surface of circumstance and desire? It would be foolish not to concede this point, for surely we have all learned from long and painful experience that there are few things less reliable than human words. Yet the recovery of dialogue today does not depend upon merely human words. It never has. For if our words enable us to build up a common *world*, if they enable us to say "we," if it is given to them to bear any fruit at all in this world, this simply reflects the fact that we are graciously allowed to participate in the creative potency of the divine *Word*. After all, we were brought into being and are at every moment preserved in existence by words that God has spoken and continues to speak. To the extent that we are enabled to wrench genuine dialogue out from under the burden of catalogue and monologue, this will only be because these divine words provide us with a place to stand and a position from which to pull. Having outlined the particular qualities of dialogue, catalogue, and monologue in the following three chapters, then, I will conclude this short study by reaffirming the majesty and efficacy of divine speech. My hope is that the words that follow will be found to be pleasing in the sight of *The Word*.

I

Dialogue

THE PREVAILING ATTITUDE TOWARD language today is *instrumentalist*. Words and speech are conceived largely as implements, the specific means by which individuals are able to represent the world to one another as well as the means by which they are able to communicate their desires and intentions to each other. Consciousness of self on this account precedes speaking, and words are taken up like tools to realize one's conscious aims. Keeping this in mind, I want to introduce the notion of dialogue by reviewing a number of observations that have been made about the nature of language, which suggest that instrumentality is less than a full description of language. For although it is true that words can be used instrumentally, language reveals itself to be far more than simply a tool or an instrument. In fact, words and speech create the very possibility of personal agency. They do so, furthermore, in terms of interpersonal relations. The *telos*, or purpose, of language, it seems, is not so much instrumental as it is *dialogical*. Indeed, words and speech do not simply make interpersonal relations possible, rather they exist for just this purpose.

Of course, we already know this. Each of us longs for the freedom to speak freely and openly to others, and each of us desires deeply to be heard and understood by others. We long for others to be honest with us about themselves. We wish that life was not so full of posturing, hypocrisy, and manipulative speech. And so, however often we are told that language is explicable simply in terms of means and ends, we know that there must be more to it. The following observations suggest that this longing is not simply wishful thinking; interpersonal communion is what words and speech are primarily for.

We begin by noting the curious difference between animal and human communication. Whereas animals are able to communicate relevant environmental information amongst themselves through a variety of signs and signals, the purpose of this communication is not to lift their awareness *out* of their environment but to sharpen and focus their awareness all the more firmly *within* it. The more completely and immediately an animal is aware of the relevant environmental information— where the food is, where dangers lie, the presence of a potential mate or rival—the better is the animal's chance of thriving within the environment. Animals are rarely absent-minded and do not ever appear to become lost in thought. Neither do they appear to be concerned, so far as we can tell, about why things have happened or what might or might not happen. Self-conscious reflection is simply not of much use to them. Rather animals are the masters of immediacy, with eyes, ears, nostrils, tongues and limbs always alert to relevant environmental information. Animal communication, by extension, tends to be spontaneous, immediate, and reflexive. At the risk of anthropomorphism, we might describe animal communication as completely unpretentious.

Human communication, by contrast, though sharing many qualities with animal communication and often serving similar purposes, extends beyond the communication of relevant environmental information into reflection about the meaning of things. Not only are we able to respond to the human cry, "Fire! Run for your life!" but we are able, after the fact, to thank those who warned us, to ponder why our lives were spared and perhaps even to resolve to live our lives differently as a result. Indeed, life may take on a whole new meaning for us on the basis of our escape. We take this ability to reflect largely for granted, but it signals a sharp departure from instinct-governed behavior, and it is only possible through uttered and/or internalized speech. We appear to be alone among the animals in our facility for symbolizing and naming our experience. This naming creates the mental space in which it becomes possible for us to reflect upon our lives. It also creates a kind of space—or, as Martin Heidegger suggests, a "clearing"—within which all of the other things that lack the power of speech can come to be seen and appreciated. Heidegger writes:

> [L]anguage is not only and not primarily an audible and written expression of what is to be communicated. It not only puts forth in words and statements what is overtly or covertly intended to be communicated; language alone brings beings as beings into the open for the first time. Where there is no language, as in the Being of a stone, plant, and animal, there is also no openness of beings, and consequently no openness of nonbeing and of the empty. Language, in naming beings for the first time, first brings beings to word and to appearance. Only this naming nominates beings *to* their Being *from out of* their Being. Such saying is a projecting of clearing, in which announcement is made of what it is that beings come into the open *as*.[1]

Although Heidegger's description of this process is perhaps somewhat opaque, at least some of the difficulty stems from the fact that we take our powers of speech for granted. We do not often consider how extraordinary these powers really are. Naming fixes a distance between ourselves and the things we name, transforming the immediacy of simple awareness into thoughtfulness and consciousness. Naming begins to situate us in a meaningful *world*.

A second observation that has been made about human speech that points to its dialogical purpose is that there are no primitive languages.[2] This is remarkable and runs entirely counter to what evolutionary biology may have led us to suspect about language as a behavior. Human languages have apparently not evolved from simple to more and more complex forms. Every known language provides, and has always provided, those who speak it with a complete system of communication.[3] The profound difference, then, between the environment of a sign-using animal and our world of speech is, as Walker Percy notes in *The Message in the Bottle*, that the former has gaps in it while the latter does not.[4] "The nonspeaking organism," Percy observes, "only notices what is relevant biologically; the speaking organism disposes of the entire horizon symbolically." Gaps in the environment that cannot be filled by way of observation and reason, Percy observes, are filled with magic and myth. Traditional man, Percy continues, has "names for edible and noxious plants; but he also has a name for all the others: 'bush.' He also 'knows' what lies beyond the horizon, what is under the earth, and where he came from."[5]

This unexpected completeness of all known languages is something of a riddle and raises interesting questions about the human place in the evolutionary scheme of things. Yet however such questions are answered, the fact that we have yet to discover a primitive language would seem to indicate that, whatever language is, it is not simply a tool that, once discovered, was subsequently refined over time and applied to more and more of our experience. Instead, language is an entire way of being in and having a *world*. We do not use language as much as we exist *in* it. Language does not have as much to do with getting things done, in other words, as it does with creating a *world* within which it becomes possible for us to think and to plan, as well to do things. Far from being mere instruments, words and speech create the framework within which instrumentality is conceivable. As Emile Benveniste notes:

> We are always inclined to that naive concept of a primordial period in which a complete man discovered another one, equally complete, and between the two of them language was worked out little by little. This is pure fiction. We can never get back to man separated from language and we shall never see him inventing it. We shall never get back to man reduced to himself and exercising his wits to conceive of the existence of another. It is a speaking man who we find in the world, a man speaking to another man, and language provides the very definition of man.[6]

A third observation about language is that the *world* it creates for us is qualified in temporal as well as spatial terms. Language makes it possible for us to say, and hence to think, "it *was*" and "it *will be*" as well as, simply, "it is." Our ability to distinguish in speech between the past, the present, and the future tenses is what makes *narration* possible. Indeed this makes meaning possible, enabling us to make sense of our lives. Language is like a lens through which we are enabled to see into an entirely new dimension and to move in time as well as in the three dimensions of space. This is one of its more remarkable features, and our understanding of ourselves and of our purposes in the *world* depends almost entirely upon it.

We can ask and attempt to answer the question of the meaning of our lives only through language, and this is only possible because language is able to situate our lives in time as well as in space. As George Steiner notes:

> Language creates: by virtue of nomination, as in Adam's naming of all forms and presences by virtue of adjective qualification, without which there can be no conceptualization of good or evil; it creates by means of predication, of chosen remembrance (all "history" is lodged in the grammar of the past tense). Above all else, language is the generator and messenger of and out of tomorrow. In root distinction from the leaf, from the animal, man alone can construct and parse the grammar of hope.[7]

The significance of the tensed quality of ordinary language becomes apparent if we contrast ordinary speech with the language of mathematics. Although mathematics is able to reckon with time as a value or variable, it cannot serve as the language of real life precisely because it cannot distinguish between past, present, and future *as possibilities*. The meaning of our lives simply cannot be expressed adequately in terms of mathematical algorithms.

And, of course, it has been observed that language is intrinsically intersubjective. The "space" created by language is inevitably social space. Words and speech are designed to be shared between speakers. Along this line, it has been noted that of the thousands of languages that we know about, not a single one of them lacks the personal pronouns *I, you, he, she,* and *it.*[8] As indicated by the adjective *personal*, these pronouns are unlike all other designations of language in that they do not refer to the idea or the concept of an individual, but to the individual him- or her- or it-*self.*[9] Moreover they lie at the very heart of speech as the *subjects* of sentences. As George Steiner observes: "A type of clause, in which a 'subject' is talked about or modified in some manner, is observable in every linguistic system. All speech operates with subject-verb-object combinations. Among these the sequences 'verb-object-subject', 'object-subject-verb', and 'object-verb-subject' are exceedingly rare. So rare, as to suggest an almost deliberate violation of a deep-rooted ordering of perception."[10] So deep-rooted is this ordering of perception, in fact, that it is all but impossible to imagine a language system in which subjects do not exercise something like personal agency as they act in a world of objects as well as other subjects. Emile Benveniste contends that the personal pronouns, and particularly the little word *I*, form the basis of subjectivity, that is, they form the basis of our experience of ourselves and others as acting agents. "We are in the presence of a class of words, the 'personal pronouns,'" Benveniste writes:

> that escapes the status of all the other signs of language. Then, what does *I* refer to? To something very peculiar which is exclusively linguistic: *I* refers to the act of individual discourse in which it is pronounced, and by this it designates the speaker. It is a term that cannot be identified except [as] an instance of discourse and that only has a momentary reference. The reality to which it refers is the reality of the discourse. It is in the instance of discourse in which *I* designates the speaker and that the speaker proclaims himself as the "subject." And so it is literally true that the basis of subjectivity is in the exercise of language. If one really thinks about it, one will see that there is no other objective testimony to the identity of the subject except that which he himself thus gives about himself.[11]

In other words, we experience ourselves as our selves when we say the word *I*. "'Ego,'" as Benveniste puts it, "is he who *says* 'ego.'"[12]

The fact that acting subjects designated by personal pronouns lie at the heart of every known language system more-or-less obviously refutes the notion that language is simply an instrument. For as we noted above, language provides the very framework within which means, ends, and agency become thinkable. To consciously take up a tool for some specific purpose is already to be conscious of oneself as a rational agent. This consciousness does not simply employ words and speech but rather it is made possible by them. Here again, it is precisely for want of words and speech that other animals appear largely incapable of rationality. As Blaise Pascal comments in the *Pensées*:

> If an animal did rationally what it does by instinct, and if it spoke rationally what it speaks by instinct when hunting, or warning its fellows that the prey has been lost, it would certainly go on to talk about matters which affect it more seriously, and it would say, for instance: "Bite through this cord; it is hurting me and I cannot reach it."[13]

We say *I*, furthermore, always and only in distinction from and in relation to a *you*. The subjectivity for which language provides a basis, in other words, is always actually intersubjective. Every act of speech is for the sake of rendering our experience of the world intelligible "for a real or implied someone else."[14] Benveniste writes:

> Consciousness of self is only possible if it is experienced by contrast. I use *I* only when I am speaking to someone who will be a *you* in my address. It is this

condition of dialogue that is constitutive of *person*, for it implies that reciprocally *I* becomes *you* in the address of the one who in his turn designates himself as *I*. Here we see a principle whose consequences are to spread out in all directions. Language is possible only because each speaker sets himself up as a *subject* by referring to himself as *I* in his discourse. Because of this, *I* posits another person, the one who, being, as he is, completely exterior to "me," becomes my echo to whom I say *you* and who says *you* to me . . . . If we seek a parallel to this, we will not find it. The condition of man in language is unique.[15]

This principle of the polarity of persons in language does, just as Benveniste comments, "spread out in all directions." Indeed, we find this to be true even when we are simply speaking to ourselves. All words, even those spoken silently to oneself, are spoken in the expectation of being heard by someone else, even if at times we must produce such a listener only in our imaginations.

Naming, in short, is for the sake of telling, and both naming and telling occur for the sake of intelligent discourse. Intelligent discourse, in turn, occurs for the sake of making shared understanding and communion possible. From this we can see that the fundamental acts of speech do not have so much to do with naming and/or predication *per se*, as if consciousness were an end-in-itself, but rather with creating the possibility of communion on the basis of a shared understanding of experience. Indeed, it is only in the midst of this shared understanding of experience, this intersubjectivity, that we come to know and to understand ourselves as subjects. As Martin Buber notes, "only through genuine intercourse with a Thou can the I of the living person be experienced as existing."[16] We come to experience and to understand ourselves only in conversations with others. The words we say to others, furthermore, contribute to their own understanding of themselves *vis-à-vis* us. Buber observes:

> Speech in its ontological sense was at all times present wherever men regarded one another in the mutuality of I and Thou; wherever one showed the other something in the world in such a way that from then on he began really to perceive it; wherever one gave another a sign in such a way that he could recognize the designated situation as he had not been able to before; wherever one communicated to the other in his own experience in such a way that it penetrated the other's circle of experience and supplemented it as from within, so that from now on his perceptions were set within a world as they had not been before. All this flowing ever again into a great stream of reciprocal sharing of knowledge—thus came to be and thus is the living We, the genuine We, which, where it fulfills itself, embraces the dead who once took part in colloquy and now take part in it through what they have handed down to posterity.[17]

In addition to making it possible to say *I* and *you*, in other words, language makes it possible for us both to say *we*. It creates the possibility of fellowship. Each of us is born into the fellowship of language, and the possibilities of our own self-understanding are nurtured within and directed by it. And having learned to speak within this fellowship of words and speech, we contribute to it for better and for worse.

The fifth and final observation that has been made about language is that the intersubjective situation created by language, within which we come to an understanding of our experience and share a *world*, is never entirely closed but always makes room for us to move freely as persons within it. The inevitable ambiguity of words, meanings, and understandings is such that the *world* which these words, meanings, and understandings build up around us, and within which we come to know and understand ourselves, is never so tightly constructed that we do not have at least a little room to speak and act freely within it. This is true even if at times it means that there is only room to remain silent and/or to withhold our consent from this *world*. This room for movement—for consent and/or dissent—is significant, for in addition to the capacity of language to create the space for our consciousness of a *world*, and in addition to the inevitable intersubjectivity of speech, the single quality that enables language to serve as the medium of truly personal existence is its *contingency*. While our lives are composed of words within language systems, they are never so unequivocally scripted that we cannot improvise upon the script and add a few lines of our own *impromptu*, as it were. In this connection, we might say that, while the great utility of mathematical language stems from the fact that it is largely unequivocal, this fit is also what accounts for its lifelessness. In mathematics, two plus two *must* equal four. Our actual experience of life, on the other hand, cannot be adequately described in terms of mathematical equations. In living speech, in short, possibility is never entirely eclipsed by necessity. We can always speak, and therefore interpret, our circumstances differently. This less-than-certain, incidental, and unpredictable quality of human language is what after all, makes it human.

Looking back at the observations we have just made about language, we can see that contingency is built into every one of them. Naming is obviously a contingent act. While the names we give things may, perhaps, be more or less adequate to them, the things do not themselves tell us how they must be named.

Rather they wait to receive their names and to come "into the open," as Heidegger puts it, on the basis of the names that we give to them. In this connection, it has been observed that a good deal of Western philosophical reflection has been directed toward the question of whether or not language reduplicates reality and, if so, how.[18] Perhaps this question has been so difficult to answer definitively because naming is a genuinely contingent act. Of course, the contingent quality of naming has been difficult to square with philosophies that do not have a place for contingency, but that is another issue that I will explain in the next chapter. For now, let us simply note that we have been granted the freedom to name those things we encounter in our experience *whatever we will*. Indeed, the Scriptures tell us that even God stood back and waited to see what Adam would name the creatures and that "*whatever* the man called each living creature, that was its name" (Gen 2:19, my emphasis). Of course, Adam's naming did not call the creatures into existence, for they existed by virtue of God's originally creative decree. Yet the sense of the text is that Adam's names were genuinely *new*, and that it was given to him to participate in the creation, if not of *the* world, then at least of a *world* of discourse that he could share with God, Eve, and eventually with his children.

Speaking of Eve, the text says that as Adam named the creatures before God he was "alone" and that "no suitable helper" was found for him among the animals. When Adam awoke to find his wife lying next to him, his exclamation, "This is now bone of my bones and flesh of my flesh!" is poignant, for we have all experienced the pain of loneliness. Yet why is Adam said to have been "alone" prior to receiving the gift of his wife, when the LORD was also there with him in the garden and the two had spoken together? Of course, on the one hand, Adam was alone because he lacked another of his own kind with whom he could obey the command to be fruitful and multiply. Yet the text would seem to indicate that Adam was also alone in the sense that he wanted another person with whom he could converse, that is, one with whom he could stand face-to-face and eye-to-eye and share the warm breath of speech. As a creature of flesh and bone Adam must have hungered for a similarly embodied and linguistically capable someone with whom he could converse. And so although the narrative does not include this, it is tempting to think that he might also have exclaimed, "Ah, here at last is someone with whom I can *talk!*"

It is also interesting to note that it was *not* given to Adam to name God, and neither was he permitted to name himself. For in the act of naming, the one who names exercises a kind of authority over that which is named. Hence only God is able to name himself and thus bring himself "into the open." All of the rest of his creatures, and even we who have been permitted to name many of the others, must *receive* names. It is only possible for us to come "into the open," it seems, on the basis of the free speech-acts of others, just as it is only possible for them to "appear" on the basis of our own contingent speech-acts.

And so the *world* comprised by speech is an inherently contingent one that can always be spoken, and hence understood, differently. This is most readily discernible in our talk about the future in which any number of things might actually happen, yet it is equally true of our talk about the past and even about the present. "Only language," George Steiner observes, "knows no conceptual, no projective finality. We are at liberty to say anything, to say what we will about anything, about everything and about nothing . . . ."[19]

Of course, if language were simply an instrument, its contingency would appear to be a serious flaw in its utility, suggesting that we might want to try somehow to purify words and speech of all ambiguity.[20] Although we will have more to say about this in our next chapter, there are those who would contend that human progress must eventually require ordinary language to be replaced by the exact mathematical language of modern science. However, were this ever actually to happen there would no longer be any room for persons to exist in our world. Those who would purify words and speech of all ambiguity fail to recognize that the room created by the contingency of words and speech is a prerequisite for truly personal existence. They also fail to recognize that the stability and reliability of our *world* does not depend upon the unequivocal sense of the words with which it is constructed as much as it depends upon the free determination of the speakers of these words to stand behind them. This is very important. Indeed, the Scriptures tell us that the stability and reliability of the created order as a whole are not qualities that are somehow built into it as much as they stem from the fact that the creation was freely *spoken* into existence by a God whose words "stand fast" because of his faithfulness; that is, because God has determined to own up to his words.

I think we can now say with some assurance that the purpose of language is not primarily instrumental but rather *dialogical.* Its purpose is not so much that of enabling us to *do* things in the world as much as it enables us to exist in a *world* within which it is possible for us to move and to act as persons, a *world* within which friendship and fellowship are real possibilities. We have discussed a few of the features of language that make such a *world* possible, i.e., the conscious distancing made possible by naming; the centrality of the personal pronouns; the completeness of language systems; the past, present, and future tenses; and the inevitable contingency of words and speech. And yet what enables our words to establish a *world* within which friendship and fellowship are possible are not these specific qualities so much as the way in which our words are spoken. As Hans Georg Gadamer notes, "[c]onversation is a process of coming to an understanding."[21] At the end of the day, the words that really make "coming to an understanding" possible for us are those that are spoken genuinely and truthfully. Communion, in other words, is not achieved simply through careful definition and articulation, but ultimately through the personal backing that each of us gives to our words as we speak them. Our words only become solid and dependable—which is to say capable of bearing the weight of a *world*—in so far as we have committed ourselves to standing behind them. Genuine communication does not require absolute unambiguity of speech. Rather it requires that each of us commit ourselves to speaking clearly, honestly, and as truthfully as we can in the interests of sharing a *world* within which we may each continue to act and speak freely as persons. William Poteat puts this very beautifully:

> [T]he heart of actual speech is the *radically* contingent, *absolutely* novel, and underivable act of owning and owning up to these my very particular words—*and this is so no matter how often it is done.* Unowned "words" are not in fact words; absconded from, they have become mere sounds—as when we say of another's empty and unowned "speech" : "words, words, words," when what we mean is of course "sounds, sounds, sounds." They are *mere* sounds, no part of language jointly owned among men; henceforth they are mere noise, surdities bereft of any human voice. Authentic speech is the act of owning my own words *before you*. Indeed, speaking authentically, that is, owning my own words before you is precisely the means of my *being a person*; to be

able to be a person is for me at bottom nothing other
than to *be* able *before you* to own my words.[22]

Poteat goes on to lament how terribly often we fail to live
up to this standard of "authentic speech" and how often we
contribute to the world's darkness and confusion by voicing
careless and/or deceitful words. Only God is as good as his
word, and it is always and only by the grace of God that we are
enabled, finally, to utter truthful words.[23]

In summary, words and speech are not merely instruments
or tools, though they may serve in an instrumental capacity.
Rather language is the medium within which the distinctively
human form of life is possible. Our words lift us out of the
immediacy of natural, instinctual existence and create space
for us to move intelligently and intentionally in a meaningful
world. Our words situate us in time as well as in space, making
it possible for us to muse upon our past as well to project
ourselves into the future. Even more basically, the little words
I, *you*, and *we* enable us to become conscious of ourselves as
responsible and personal agents. As we address each other in
words and speech, owning up to our words before each other,
we are enabled to enter into friendship and fellowship. The
medium of *spirituality*, which is to say spirited and "response-
able" existence, in short, is *dialogue*. Through dialogue we are
enabled to love God, to love our neighbors as ourselves, and to
care for the world. Where dialogue is realized, Martin Buber
comments, "between partners who have turned to one another
in truth, who express themselves without reserve and are
free of the desire for semblance, there is brought into being a
memorable common fruitfulness which is to be found nowhere
else."[24] The give and take of dialogue is the heart that beats at
the center of life.

Conditions for Genuine Dialogue

What, then, are the conditions for genuine dialogue? At the very least dialogue requires us to be situated together within a common *world* and to be able, somehow, to hear each other speak. Of course, face-to-face interaction is almost always preferable in this regard, and yet people have shown themselves to be remarkably adept at creating the space for spoken interaction even at great distances. Dialogue further requires us to share a more-or-less common dictionary and grammar. Although certain conventions for telling each other things appear to be almost universally recognized—smiling, grimacing, shaking one's head, pointing at things, etc.—dialogue will be rather limited for those who do not speak each other's language. And even if we do share a common tongue our dialogue may be impeded, for a time at least, by the specialized vocabularies and varying grammatical conventions that increasingly characterize modern social life.

Yet the principal conditions for fruitful dialogue remain rather simple. One of them is that, as we speak to each other—however and under whatever conditions we manage to do this—we recognize that the *you* to whom we say *I* is also a living, acting personal subject in his or her own right.[25] Dialogue, as the Golden Rule suggests, requires us to speak and to listen to others just as we would have them speak and listen to us. We all know well enough how often our words are presumptuous, prejudiced, or simply mistaken, yet we still want to be heard. We hope that grace will be extended to us as we speak and that we might, in spite of everything, be heard as persons. Entering into dialogue requires us to extend just this kind of grace to others. In short, it presupposes *respect*. Dialogue requires us to listen carefully to others and to take care regarding the words we speak to them out of respect for who they are. As Buber writes:

> Genuine conversation, and therefore every actual fulfil-
> lment of relation between [people], means acceptance
> of otherness. When two [people] inform one another
> of their basically different views about an object, each
> aiming to convince the other of the rightness of [their]
> own way of looking at the matter, everything depends
> so far as human life is concerned, on whether each
> thinks of the other as the one he [or she] is, whether
> each, that is, with all [their] desire to influence the
> other, nevertheless unreservedly accepts and confirms
> [the other] in [their] being this [person] and in [their]
> being made in this particular way.[26]

In addition to listening to others as they are, dialogue requires us to speak as *we* are and not as we might perhaps prefer to appear.[27] Such honesty and openness always entails risk, and sometimes considerable risk, for there is no guarantee that the others to whom we speak will open themselves to us or that they will appreciate who we are. Indeed, much of our experience probably suggests that they will not and hence that it is far safer to project an image of ourselves than to allow ourselves to appear as we are. Yet if we use our words to project images back and forth to each other, then whatever else we may accomplish in such an exchange, it cannot be said that we have managed to come to any real understanding. And while this kind of virtual dialogue may well be the norm in our world today, it does not nourish or sustain us, at least not for very long. After all, we do not want merely to *seem* to have fellowship with one another, which is all that these virtual conversations manage to accomplish. We long for real fellowship. We do not simply want to *seem* to have friends, but to really have them.

"Whatever the meaning of the word 'truth' may be in other realms," Buber notes, "in the interhuman realm it means that [people] communicate themselves to one another as what they are.[28] Of course, this does not mean that absolutely everything must be said in each and every conversation, but it does mean allowing each other genuine access to ourselves. Where this access is denied, there can be no dialogue.

In addition to resisting the temptation to allow pretense to creep in between us, we must stand behind the words we speak and own up to them after we have uttered them. For, as we have seen, it is only as we own up to our words that the *world* created by these words comes to be solid, dependable, and livable. Naturally, this is most obviously true of the promises we make to each other and of our commitments to be and to do things for each other. Along this line, I am the father of four children, and I am all too aware of how precariously their *world* rests upon the promises I have made to my wife. Not only does their *world* hang on these promises at present, but their ability to make similar promises in the future and to establish a dependable *world* for their children is also linked to my and my wife's commitment to stand, by the grace of God, behind the words we said to each other almost thirty years ago in a small church in Northern California. That we have managed to do so is in no small measure due to the perseverance our parents had in holding to words that they spoke to each other before my wife and I were born.

Yet dialogue does not simply require us to stand behind our explicit promises, but behind all the other words we speak as well, for we will eventually be called to give account for all of them. In the meantime, owning up to our words before each other means, as Christ commanded, letting our "yes" be *yes* and our "no" be *no*. Of course, this is not to say that we may venture to speak only if we know that our words are absolutely accurate and wholly adequate to the truth of things. For although we strive for accuracy and clarity in our speech, being mistaken does not necessarily undermine fruitful conversation. To err, after all, is human and, as the Apostle James observes (Jas 3:2), only one who is perfect is "never at fault in what he says." To the extent that we find ourselves at fault in what we say, it is also important to recall that words are remarkably powerful healing agents. They are just as able to restore us to fellowship with one another as they are able to disrupt this fellowship. "Pleasant words," Proverbs 16:24 states, "are a honeycomb, sweet to the soul and healing to the bones." And so the "truth" most requisite for dialogue is not that of absolute accuracy, but of fidelity, constancy, sincerity, and honesty, the sort of things implied when we say that someone is a *true* friend. Indeed, in this connection we note that our word "truth" evolved from the Old English word *treowth*, from which the word "betrothal" is also taken. On the other hand, and as we will discuss in more detail, diffidence, double-mindedness, and deceitfulness always undermine dialogue. If you and I cannot depend upon the words that we speak to each other—if one or both of us is ignorant, careless, or less-than-truthful—then we will never come to the kind of understanding that will enable us to move forward together in fellowship. Our words will have become, at best, obstacles to fellowship and perhaps even hazards to our lives.

Finally, for our conversations to be truly fruitful, we must be committed, in principle, to seeking out the truth of things and to speaking in such a way that the truth of things may be seen and, even more importantly, may be heard. Indeed, our words will only serve to edify and build up to the extent that they point toward the truth of things.

Now, to say this is to assume that the truth of things is, finally, intelligible and also that it is good, and therefore good for us to seek and to talk about. This is not an assumption to be taken lightly. For to doubt the underlying intelligibility and goodness of things gives way almost immediately to a loss of confidence in words and speech. Where this happens, the question of fruitful dialogue as we have framed it is not likely even to arise. We will return to this point in a moment.

It is important to stress here that the commitment to seeking out the truth of things need never be severe and coercive. In respecting the freedom of others in dialogue, we must allow them the freedom to see and hear differently, the freedom to err, and even the freedom not to see and hear at all. Nevertheless, we cannot simply for the sake of civility back away from seeking out the larger meaning of things. It is tempting to do so today, for modern society and culture are largely built upon the premise that meaning is simply something that we construct for ourselves *de novo*. Yet to give in to this temptation, and to restrict our conversations simply to the practical exigencies of the here and now, we must eventually find that we have very little to say to each other about good, evil, death, justice, and host of other pressing matters. If we do not seriously concern ourselves with the matter of truth, in other words, our words must eventually devolve into chatter.

Why Dialogue Breaks Down

Dialogue may break off or break down for any number of reasons. In the first instance, speakers may not be situated in such a way as to be able to hear or understand one another. This may be due to the fact that they do not share a common language or a common *world* of discourse. Dialogue may also break off because interlocutors are not given the room to move into new ideas and positions. There can be no real dialogue, after all, where there is no respect for others as persons, which, we note, is frequently the case. While many of our interactions may appear to be dialogical, we may not actually be listening to and addressing each other. In fact, we are always in danger of using each other simply as occasions for listening to ourselves. "By far the greater part of what is today called conversation among men," Buber comments, "would be more properly and precisely described as speechifying. In general, people do not really speak to one another, but each, although turned to the other, really speaks to a fictitious court of appeal whose life consists of nothing but listening to him."[29] The clearest mark of this kind of person, he continues, is that he cannot really listen to the voice of another. "[I]n all his hearing, as in all his seeing, he mixes observation. The other is not the man over against him whose claim stands over against his own in equal right; the other is only his object."[30]

Beyond using each other, in effect, as sounding boards for listening to ourselves, we also use each other with other purposes in mind. Pretense, hypocrisy, and other verbal strategies that fall under the heading of *seeming* are the enemies of dialogue, as, of course, are deceitfulness and duplicity. Obviously, it is impossible to enter into a dialogue with someone whom we have already rendered as an object and whom we approach not with the intention of listening, but only of using.

Yet it is also important to stress that in addition to denying others' freedom to speak, we may also deny or surrender our own freedom to speak by refusing to take ourselves seriously or by trying to evade responsibility for our words. Perhaps we are afraid to be called to account for our words, and so we flee into the anonymity and irresponsibility of the crowd, where our words can no longer be distinguished as *our* words and we cannot be held responsible for uttering them.[31] Søren Kierkegaard, in 1846, contended that this kind of despairing irresponsibility was the hallmark of his age. "Each age has its own characteristic depravity," he commented.

> Ours is perhaps not pleasure or indulgence or sensuality, but rather a dissolute pantheistic contempt for the individual man. In the midst of all of our exultation over the achievements of the age . . . , there sounds a note of poorly conceived contempt for the individual man; in the midst of the self-importance of the contemporary generation there is revealed a sense of despair over being human. Everything must attach itself so as to be a part of some movement; men are determined to lose themselves in the totality of things, in world-history, fascinated and deceived by a magic witchery; no one wants to be an individual human being.[32]

While we postmoderns may no longer exult over the achievements of the modern age, and although indulgence and sensuality do appear to be rather significant themes in contemporary culture, the "sense of despair over being human" appears to be as much of a problem today as it was in mid-nineteenth-century Denmark. Nowhere is this more evident, it seems to me, than in the carelessness with which words are thrown about these days.

Dialogue must also eventually break down in the absence of any kind of commitment to discovering and giving voice to the truth of existence. As we noted at the outset, we inevitably find ourselves desiring to know *what* we are in relation to things, *where* we are in time, *how* we have come to be here, and, ultimately, *who* we are. Words and speech enable us together to seek to answer such questions. To leave off seeking to answer them is to ensure that our words must eventually become hollow and empty. While we may still appreciate the importance of words and speech for fellowship, despairing over the possibility of discovering the meaning of human existence means that we must eventually either fall silent or, as is more commonly the case, we must fill the world with more and more noise.

Fear and mistrust always seem to lie at the root of the breaking off of dialogue. We see this in the Genesis account when, after having eaten of the forbidden fruit, the first man and the first woman try to hide from the Creator's *voice*. Indeed, from almost the very beginning, it seems that our species has run into difficulties with dialogue. It is still the case that most of our words are arrogant or foolish, spoken without true understanding. To the extent that we have managed to enjoy fruitful conversations with each other this has only been—and will always be—by God's grace. This would have been true even if the first man and woman had not been expelled from the garden. For all meaningful speech must echo, however dimly and distantly it does so at present, the *original Words* that brought forth and continue to uphold the created order.[33]

Having said all this, however, we need to be aware that the conviction that it is still possible, in spite of everything, to speak truthfully and meaningfully to each other has come under attack in recent times. Skeptical theorists have observed that the very words truth, justice, freedom, responsibility, and many others cannot be uttered without implying the existence of One who underwrites their meaning. Contending that such a One does not exist, such theorists have insisted that we must put all such words—indeed, *all* words—in inverted commas. "Truth," "justice," "freedom," "responsibility," so the argument goes, are empty or, at best, only convenient fictions. They are simply verbal tools that have been used and are still being used in the interests of those in positions of power. "Truths," Nietzsche insisted, for example, "are illusions which we have forgotten are illusions, worn out metaphors now impotent to stir the senses, coins which have lost their faces and are considered now as metal rather than currency."[34] That such words continue to work and to move us, according to Nietzsche, is simply an indication that we have failed to realize that "God is dead."

Perhaps recent theorists cannot be blamed for being suspicious of human words, for there are few things that are less reliable. Yet it is important to stress that at least a few of the critics are not simply suspicious of human words but appear, following Nietzsche, to doubt the possibility of truthful speech altogether.[35] Radically doubting the underlying intelligibility and goodness of things, it seems, has led inevitably to a loss of confidence in words and speech. Of course, were such postmodern skeptics correct, dialogue would not simply be rare in practice, it would be impossible in principle. If our words are always and only implements, and if they are voiced as means to the end of advancing our own individual interests, then whatever shared understanding we may happen to enjoy will simply be the result of the coincidence of our interests and not of our having entered into dialogue. Even more to the point, if words are always and only employed for the sake of advancing selfish interests, then there is really no point in raising the subjects of dialogue, coming to an understanding, or fellowship, for they are all illusory. Thank God, then, that the skeptics are mistaken. Yet given popular perceptions—and misperceptions—of the program of "deconstructing" all claims to truth, and given the fact that so many today have become increasingly cynical with respect to words and speech, it is perhaps not surprising that dialogue has been eclipsed by the impersonal speech of catalogue and by the manipulative words of monologue.

Dialogue, Human Origins, and Human Destiny

We have said that human origins and human destiny are both bound up with dialogue. With respect to the former, it is interesting that evolutionary biologists have found that the only characteristic that distinguishes us from other animals is our curious ability to speak.[36] The gap separating our capacity for verbal symbolization from that of our nearest evolutionary relatives, the great apes, is so large and appeared so suddenly that it has naturally called for explanation. While many researchers continue to assert that our capacity for speech must somehow have evolved along conventional Darwinian lines— i.e., that speech must somehow have conferred upon our species some kind of evolutionary advantage and must, therefore, have been naturally selected—others have suggested that the human brain's extraordinary ability to process words and speech may actually have evolved for reasons that had nothing to do with language as such. Along this line, Harvard biologist Stephen Jay Gould has coined the term "spandrel" to describe the accidental appearance of a biological structure or capacity that, while having developed in the conventional Darwinian fashion, is subsequently and suddenly put to an entirely new and different use, resulting in the unexpected appearance of a new capacity and a new form of life. Language's sudden appearance on the evolutionary stage, Gould argues, may well be explicable along such lines. "Yes, the brain got big by natural selection . . . ," Gould writes:

> [but] the brain did not get big so that we could read or write or do arithmetic or chart the seasons—yet human culture, as we know it, depends upon skills

of this kind . . . . [T]he universals of language are so different from anything else in nature, and so quirky in their structure, that origin as a side consequence of the brain's enhanced capacity, rather than as a simple advance in continuity from ancestral grunts and gestures, seems indicated.[37]

Now, although Gould is, perhaps, not the most obvious authority to cite given our interest in defending the spirituality of speaking and listening, his observation is an interesting one, and it is one that is not altogether impossible to square with biblical understanding. After all, given what we have said about the dialogical *telos* of language, we would not expect words and speech to have emerged mechanically out of a biological capacity *per se*. For although we must obviously be biologically fit to speak, dialogue—and hence consciousness—can only emerge out of a personal address, that is, when one is addressed as a *Thou* by another who says *I*. There does not, furthermore, appear to be any graduated way in which this can happen. A proto-*I* cannot engage a proto-*Thou* in a kind of almost-but-not-quite personal fashion. Rather dialogue is an all-or-nothing event. Either it occurs in the fullness of interpersonal relation or it does not occur at all.

Perhaps we can employ this insight to shed some light on the knotty question of human origins. For although we will never know what the first truly human words spoken were, I think they might have been something like, "Yes, I am well. Thank you." They might, in other words, have been awakened by the simple question, uttered by God, perhaps in the silence of his creature's heart, "Adam. Are you alright?" Obviously, this is pure speculation, but given the perplexing difficulties religious believers have had in trying to defend human singularity on the basis of some kind of natural capacity, would it not be enough to say that we human beings are the creatures that God has *called* into "response-ability"? Would it not be enough to say that the first human person—*Adam*, the child of the earth—was first simply by virtue of having been been invited into responsible dialogue with the living, speaking God? Certainly everything that we know about the singularity of language and about the specific qualities of spoken interaction would seem to point in this direction. Now, it is true that the Genesis account does not tell us how God created the first man, but simply that he did so, and that, having named him, he conversed with him in the garden. And evolutionary biology, for its part, will never uncover the words that brought the first human being into full self-consciousness. Yet it is intriguing how closely the coming-to-be of humankind and the coming-to-be of speech appear to have coincided.[38]

If human origins can be tied to dialogue, then so, too, can the matter of human destiny. With the first gift of the divine address to us we were endowed with the capacity to respond as persons to our Creator, to name the other creatures, and to converse with one another. "The sign of this communication of life," Nelly Villianeix has commented, following Søren Kierkegaard, "is only a 'small' word, but which speaks all: *tak*, thank you."[39] And so just as we can imagine that the small words "thank you" might have been the first fully human words to have been uttered, so continuing to say these small words is, Christianly speaking, our destiny. The *Westminster Larger Catechism*, for example, queries: "What is the chief and highest end of man?" and then answers: "Man's chief and highest end is to glorify God, and fully to enjoy him for ever."[40] Although the prospect of enjoying God forever is astounding it is nevertheless understandable that we might well do so, but I have often wondered, perhaps in part simply because the term is so rarely used today, what it might mean to "glorify" him forever. It will undoubtedly mean a great many things, but one of them surely must be that we will continually *thank* him. We will thank him for his graciousness and goodness to us, and for inviting us into conversation. Along this line, I would think that we anticipate our "chief and highest end" every time we behold something beautiful and find that after we have exclaimed, "Ah, how wonderful!" we are almost compelled to say "Thank you!" Our destiny is to say these small words forever and so to experience the gratitude that is the perfection of happiness.

Just as the matters of origins and destiny are bound up with dialogue, so the destruction of dialogue poses an elemental threat to our being at present and to temporal happiness. The world that has been given to us to name, tell about, and love was from the very beginning a *world* of words and speech, first of God's words, but also of the words uttered freely and contingently by the first human creatures. The thickness and consistency of this original world was underwritten by the trustworthiness and faithfulness of the divine speaker, but it remained to be seen if the first human creatures would choose to remain within it and to commit themselves obediently to the divine command. It is no wonder, then, that the enemy began to try to unmake this first world by playing with words and specifically by intimating that God's words might actually be less than wholly trustworthy. "Did God *really* say . . . ?" the serpent began (Gen 3:1,4), and then concluded the original temptation with a half-truth, "You will not surely die. . . ." Tragically, the serpent managed to deceive our first parents, thereby introducing death, corruption, and the distortion of language into our world. Yet what remains of our world's thickness and consistency is still underwritten by the trustworthiness and faithfulness of the speakers of words. Refusing to take words seriously or deceitfully playing with them is still the surest way to confuse and to unmake our world.

2

Catalogue

IN AN INTRIGUING ESSAY entitled "The Message in the Bottle," novelist Walker Percy tells of a man who finds himself castaway on the shore of a remote island civilization.[1] The castaway is aware that his real home lies somewhere across the sea, but he does not know where, and he cannot recall how he came to be left on the island. The islanders are of little help to him in these regards, for they know of no other place than their island. The castaway is, nonetheless, welcomed into island society and soon, as Percy writes, "he makes the best of the situation, gets a job, builds a house, takes a wife, raises a family, goes to night school, and enjoys the local arts of cinema, music, and literature. He becomes, as the phrase goes, a useful member of the community."[2]

The castaway is an avid beachcomber, for he has noticed that glass bottles occasionally wash ashore and that some of these bottles have messages in them. He takes an interest in these messages because he hopes that one of them may, someday, contain some clue as to where he came from and, hence, who he is. Yet he finds that most of the messages are bits of scientific information, matters of fact, apparently historical reports related to island life, or other scraps of information that, although occasionally useful, have nothing to do with his quest for identity.

As much as the castaway learns about life on the island and as settled and pleasant as his life is, the critical *existential* question he faces remains: "Where have I come from?" If he cannot somehow answer this question, he will never succeed—as happy and as well adjusted as he may otherwise be—in knowing himself. The castaway must be extremely careful, then, not to mistake the various bits of knowledge he happens across on the island—whether this knowledge is gained empirically, as by the methods of science, or whether this knowledge relates simply to the particular social history of the islanders—for knowledge that is genuinely relevant to his existential quest. He must not, in other words, allow himself to forget that the only knowledge *existentially* relevant to him must somehow come from "across the sea." He must also take care not to become complacent or get to the point where he feels so at home on the island that he leaves off trying to find out where he has come from. If he thus becomes complacent, he will have lost himself. Percy writes:

> Then what should he do? It is not for me to say here that he do this or that or should believe such and such. But one thing is certain. He should be what he is and not pretend to be somebody else. He should be a castaway and not pretend to be at home on the island. To be a castaway is to be in a grave predicament and this is not a happy state of affairs. But it is very much happier than being a castaway and pretending one is not. This is despair. The worst of all despairs is to imagine one is at home when one is really homeless.[3]

Percy's is, of course, a Christian parable intended to encourage us to consider whether we are not also "castaway" in this world and to consider the possibility that our origin and destiny may somehow mysteriously transcend that which is visible to us at the present. If this is the case then the only kind of knowledge that can really speak to the matters of *identity* and *existence*—*Where* are we? *How* did we get here? *Who* are we really? *What* is our ultimate destiny?—must come to us, first, as genuine "news"—that is, as opposed to any kind of knowledge (say, scientific knowledge) that can, in principle, be discovered by anyone at any time simply by carefully examining our present circumstances—and, second, as "news from across the sea"—that is, the news must be distinguishable from all of the news generated about mere happenings in this world. Furthermore, in order for us to recognize that this "news from across the sea" is existentially relevant, we must be seeking after it. We must not have become so comfortable in this world that we have allowed ourselves to forget that we are castaways. In this connection Percy makes an important distinction between what he calls "the posture of the castaway"—that is, the posture of one who retains the memory of having first found himself on the island and still searches for clues as to where he came from—and "the posture of objectivity," in which one settles simply for describing island life and for adapting oneself to it as completely and as comfortably as possible. While adopting the latter posture may well result more immediately in a greater sense of well-being it exacts a high price existentially, for then the castaway will never really know who he is.

And so it is that we must seek to distinguish between genuine, existentially relevant *revelation* and all of the lesser revelations produced by our scientific and technological culture. We must be careful not to confuse the knowledge that modern secular culture produces—as marvelous and as useful as it is—for knowledge that is genuinely relevant to our existential predicament. We must also take care not to become complacent and not to give up searching out the matter of our destiny. As Kierkegaard once observed, "It is not entirely impossible that one who is infinitely interested in his eternal happiness may sometime come into possession of it. But it is surely quite impossible for one who has lost a sensibility for it (and this can scarcely be anything else than the infinite interest), ever to enjoy an eternal happiness. If the sense for it is once lost, it may perhaps be impossible to recover it."[4]

Unfortunately, culture often stands in the way of our existential quest. Modern secular culture in particular has a way of persuading us that this world is really all there is, that it contains all we can possibly need, and hence that scientific and/or this-worldly knowledge is all we require in the construction of more-or-less normal identities. Indeed, from the perspective of secularity—a word taken from the Latin term, *saeculum*, or "this age"—adopting the posture of the castaway and taking an infinite interest in eternal happiness is irrational, even absurd. For it threatens to undermine our experience of well-being here and now by reminding us that we are not at home and that the current state of affairs is not—and can never be—an entirely satisfactory one. As one contributor to *The New York Times* contended several years ago, "The idea that there is such a thing as an eternal life and that it is in most ways more important than this life . . . has generally caused immensely greater misery than it has helped the world."[5] Of course, such an observation is quite correct in one sense. For the idea of an eternal life, as Nietzsche saw clearly, does indeed pose a principal threat to the present age.[6]

My reason for citing Percy's parable of the castaway here at the outset of our second chapter is that it provides a useful introduction to a kind of speech that I want to discuss under the heading of "catalogue." Using Percy's terms, catalogue speech is that which is spoken out of a posture of objectivity. It is the kind of speech that makes up much of what passes for knowledge today. It is largely descriptive and aims to be objective. It can be quite sophisticated and is very often useful. It is the language most of us spend many years in school learning to speak, particularly in universities and graduate schools. It is the kind of speech that has been heralded most recently as "information" and which is supposed, by means of information technology, to usher us into a new era of comfort and convenience. Indeed, the cataloguing of objective knowledge—both in words and images—is something we have become quite adept at in modern times. Yet because so much of our catalogued knowledge is—or at least tries to be—objective, which is to say factual, analytic, and descriptive, it is not really able to speak to the questions of *existence*. Produced in sufficient quantities, furthermore, catalogue knowledge can render us altogether insensitive to the question of destiny and indifferent to the possibility of eternal happiness. Indeed, Kierkegaard believed that this is precisely what had happened in nineteenth-century Denmark, and it moved him to write polemically against the modern age. "My principal [concern]," Kierkegaard reflected, "was that in our age, because of the great increase of knowledge, we had forgotten what it means to *exist*, and what *inwardness* signifies."[7]

Beyond failing to speak to the matter of existence, catalogue speech also fails to address us personally. It is strangely anonymous speech, not really uttered by an *I* and not really addressed to a *you*. This is perhaps why it is so readily transmissible by machines and machine technology. Instead of inviting us into dialogue, the words of catalogue present us with a useful but oddly dissociated compendium of descriptions and indications of objects, events, and processes. To use the terms that we introduced earlier, catalogue presents us with an overabundance of names, but it doesn't really tell us anything about ourselves at the deepest level or about what it means to exist. Indeed, a great many of the words that reach our eyes and ears today fail—either because they are spoken out of the posture of objectivity or because they are not addressed to us personally—to situate us in existence. As useful as many of these words are, they fail to establish a meaningful *world* within which it is possible for us to discover who we are, to become ourselves in relation to others, and to begin to apprehend wisdom, which is to say the truth about the larger meaning of things. Of course, for the most part, these words are not intentionally depersonalizing, as the words of monologue are, yet neither do they enable us to become persons, as the words of dialogue do. Rather the term that best describes the peculiar quality of catalogue speech is that it is *impersonal.* It is often interesting, informative, and very often useful, but it seems to reach only into the surface levels of the intellect, which is perhaps why the term "intellectual" is not commonly associated with wisdom.

Admittedly, *catalogue* is not quite the right term to place in between *dialogue* and *monologue* on the continuum of attitudes that it is possible to take with respect to words and speech. Unlike the words "dialogue" and "monologue," "catalogue" does not derive from the Greek "logos" (word) and does not really refer to speech at all. Rather it derives from the Greek "kata" (from, down) and "legein" (to choose) and denotes "to reckon in a list" or "to classify."[8] Our ordinary use of the term suggests as much, for catalogues are typically informative lists or collections of information like library catalogues, dictionaries, and encyclopedias, as well as listings of goods and services. Catalogues are also almost always typographical and graphical phenomena. Their utility lies in the fact that they order things visually and enable us to *see* things arranged in order. To the extent that we are able to locate things quickly and to see them arranged in order, we are thereby enabled to work with and manage them more efficiently and effectively.

Considered as a kind of speech, catalogue supplies us with potentially useful information. Just as ordinary catalogues are visual tools, so catalogue speech tends to be visually biased, which is to say it is largely descriptive. Its purpose is to enable us to *see* things as clearly as possible, particularly the surface relations between things. Considered as an attitude, catalogue derives principally from—and leads primarily to—a posture of *observation*. It entails standing back away from things and reckoning them into lists and systems. From the perspective of catalogue, then, while words are valued to the extent that they are accurate and useful, the thickness and consistency of the world is not understood to hinge in any meaningful way upon the personal backing that words receive. Rather, words are principally understood to be indications, and their value derives from the accuracy of the observations on which they are based. Catalogue words announce what is already the case with the world, often preparing us for practical activity within it. To speak out of the posture of catalogue is not to speak in an active voice, but rather indicatively and passively, as if to say, "It is the case that . . ." or "It is found that . . . ."

Recalling Percy's parable, we might say that catalogue speech is like all the bits of scientific and island news the castaway finds scattered along the beach—informative and pragmatically useful, but essentially irrelevant to our existential predicament. Expanding the parable somewhat, we might say that our predicament in this world is not simply that we do not know where we have come from, but also that we do not know who left us here and why. Without knowing these things, we cannot know who we are. We cannot, to put the matter most pointedly, know our *names*. What we desperately need, then, is not island news or information, indeed not even "news from across the sea," *per se*, but to receive a message, some kind of correspondence personally addressed to us by someone who knows us by name. Short of receiving such a message, and finding ourselves increasingly deluged only by more and more knowledge and more and more information, we are in grave danger of lapsing into despair and of giving up hope of ever being able to discover who we really are.

The Visual Bias of Modern Thought

Intriguingly, the modern age stands apart from all others in its preference for the largely impersonal words and speech of catalogue over those of dialogically spoken wisdom. Perhaps this is because we have come to understand knowledge and knowing—perhaps more thoroughly than any other culture ever has before—in terms of sight and seeing. We have, in a sense, become convinced that seeing really is believing and that to see things ordered in visual space is to know all that there really is to know about them. Just as the practical utility of a catalogue lies in its capacity for arranging things visually and typographically, so we have come to believe that if we can see the surface relations between things, we can be said to know them completely. This could be why we have come to place such a high value upon knowledge and upon ways of knowing that are based upon visualization.

Here we might recall the adage that "a picture is worth a thousand words." The phrase is interesting because it is often recited, and yet it is only actually true of a rather limited range of largely practical matters. I would, for example, rather hear my beloved's voice or receive a letter from her than simply look at her photograph. Indeed, if we were forced to endure a long separation I believe I would gladly trade a thousand photographs of her for five minutes of conversation with her. In the case of personal relationships, pictures, though valuable, are never so valuable as a thousand words. Rather it seems that pictures are only worth more than words when it comes to practical actions involving complicated physical shapes and movements.[9] When I want to drive to a place that I haven't been to before, for example, I would much rather rely on a map or a diagram than simply upon verbal instructions. If I am forced to rely upon verbal instructions, furthermore, they must be clear and detailed enough to enable me to visualize where I must go. When I need to fix something mechanically, I hope that someone might be able to show me how to go about it, or at least that the operation will be pictured and not simply described in my owner's manual. The common assertion that a "picture is worth a thousand words" is true, then, but only so long as we are interested primarily in understanding the spatial relations between things or when we are trying to effect practical changes involving more-or-less complex shapes or movements. Picturing things, in short, is crucial only when it comes to practical or technical understanding. As Marshall McLuhan observed, "[T]he key to any kind of *applied* knowledge is the translation of a complex of relations into explicit visual terms."[10] "All techniques," as Jacques Ellul noted similarly (following Oswald Spengler), "are based on visualization and involve visualization. If a phenomenon cannot be transformed into something visual, it cannot be the object of a technique."[11]

If cataloguing things entails arranging them spatially and visually for the sake of practical action, this would suggest that a visual bias ought to characterize any society known for its practical and technical proficiency. And indeed it does characterize modern technological society. The ascendancy of catalogue speech today appears to stem from the tremendous emphasis we have placed upon trying to effect practical control over our circumstances by means of a sort of descriptive analysis that hinges upon our ability to visualize things. In a sense we appear to have become convinced that if we can only accumulate enough information about how the world is constructed and how it works, this accumulation will enable us to make the world work for us, and this will perhaps enable us to discover who we are. We appear, as a culture, to have ruled out the possibility that our existence may not, finally, be explicable in terms of present circumstances and appearances.

The visualization of cognition and the emphasis we have come to place upon cataloguing knowledge have deep roots within the Western tradition, which may be traced all the way back to the Greek philosophical imagination. We will need to explore these specific roots in some detail below, but it should be noted at the outset that philosophical reasoning is perhaps always biased in the direction of visualization simply because it is interested in seeing the truth of things put in order. Martin Buber observed, for example, "[a]ll great religiousness shows us that the reality of faith means living in relationship to Being 'believed in,' that is, unconditionally affirmed, absolute Being, [a]ll great philosophy . . . shows us that cogitative truth means making the absolute into an object from which all other objects must be derived."[12] The peculiarly visual bias characterizing contemporary culture is remarkable, however, and calls for further interpretation. The first thing to say along this line is that our visual bias is one of the more significant indications that Western philosophy has indeed, as Whitehead is said to have quipped, been a series of footnotes to Plato.

Within the Platonic tradition the universe is not personally encountered—as when one encounters another in dialogue—as much as it is "beheld." The universe is "pictured," as it were, as closed, static, finite, and grounded ultimately in an eternal and impersonal principle of being, or *Logos*. The metaphors and models that best represent our knowledge of what is, then, are visual and spatial, and the object of philosophy is passively to behold what is eternal, immutable, and at rest. Ultimately, all of this becomes visible only through the theoretical intuition of the "mind's eye."[13] Yet words and speech may serve as secondary, derivative, and more-or-less fallible instruments for communicating what one has intuitively "seen."[14] From such a perspective (note the word!), words and speech are not understood to establish the order of things as much as they may, if the speaker is disciplined and rational, enable us to begin to see and to comprehend how things have been ordered. Whatever effectiveness words possess in communicating the order of things, furthermore, has very little to do with their spokenness or with their having been spoken by someone who owns them or stands behind them. Indeed, the contingent quality of ordinary speech is held to be an impediment to philosophical reflection. Rather the value of words lies in their capacity for re-presenting the truth of things reasonably and in order.[15] Not surprisingly, the language often thought best suited to philosophical contemplation has been that of mathematics, for mathematical language appears largely immune to the ambiguity, contingency, and accidental quality of ordinary speech.[16] The ideal toward which the philosophical imagination strives, however, is ultimately wordless, for it is simply to envision the eternal order of things and to lose oneself in contemplative wonder. The Greek philosophical imagination is one for which the term "worldview" is entirely apposite.

It is worth noting that the Platonic imagination, with its strong emphasis upon abstract theoretical visualization, is unusual by comparison with other Oriental cultures, which tended to place more emphasis upon dynamic spoken interaction and spoken wisdom, and which often interpreted the world in terms of a pantheon of "gods" who quarreled and occasionally cooperated with each other more-or-less as we do.[17] Interestingly, Walter Ong, Marshall McLuhan, and others have suggested that the mental discipline required to abstract timeless philosophical truths from the dynamism of ordinary experience, and away from the contingency of ordinary spoken interaction, may actually have depended upon a kind of technological breakthrough: the development of the phonetic alphabet.

While not a Greek invention *per se*, the Greeks appeared to have put the phonetic alphabet to good philosophical use, and not simply in recording their arguments and systems. More importantly the alphabet seems to have been the lens through which Greek thinkers learned, in effect, to see through the clutter of ordinary experience and, by means of abstract symbolization, to *envision* and to represent the eternal order of things. "Only the phonetic alphabet," McLuhan asserts, "makes a break between eye and ear, between semantic meaning and visual code; and thus only phonetic writing has the power to translate man from the tribal to the civilized [i.e., rational] sphere, to give him an eye for an ear."[18] Furthermore, McLuhan insists that the extent to which the Greeks managed to espouse an essentially new kind of abstract and rational picture of the world may well have been because they had already formed the mental habit of manipulating the abstract symbols of the phonetic alphabet and had thus begun to learn how to arrange ideas visually, sequentially, logically, and rationally.

Yet however the origins of the Greek philosophical imagination are interpreted, its decidedly visual bias became an
important component of Western culture and one that resurfaced
dramatically in the seventeenth-century in the development
of early-modern science. Of course, just how and why this
happened has been the subject of some debate, for modern
scientific visualization is empirical and not at all concerned to
look *past* our actual experience to a world of Platonic "Forms."
Science does not expect to see through things to the light of the
eternal *Logos*; it simply hopes to illuminate the order of things
by shining the light of disciplined intellect upon them. Rather
than cultivating reflection and contemplation, then, modern
science fosters activism and manipulation. Its aim, as René
Descartes put it at the outset of the modern period, is to render
us "the masters and possessors of nature."[19] There are rather
significant differences between modernity's visual bias and its
philosophical antecedent. Still, the modern scientific outlook is
largely visually biased.

This epistemological bias in the direction of sight and
seeing can perhaps be understood as an amalgamation of the
perennially attractive philosophical tendency to equate knowing
with seeing and the Christian—and particularly Protestant—
doctrine of creation. Created order, the Reformers affirmed, is
undeniably rational and intelligible but also wholly contingent.
God was not bound to create the world in any particular
fashion and the world is not an extension of or emanation from
his being. Hence the only way to truly know the created order
is not to speculate about how it ought to be ordered, given what
Christian theology affirms to be true about God, but instead
to go out into the world and to see how God has actually
ordered it. When it came to speaking about the order perceived
in this way, Protestant researchers understandably resorted

to philosophically conditioned visual metaphors and visual analogies. To think God's thoughts after him, as Newton is said to have described the scientific task, was in effect to strive to *see* the world as we imagine that God might see it, to stand entirely outside of the world and to observe it *sub species aeternitatis*.

Protestant thinkers also held the pursuit of scientific knowledge as an ethical duty, for they believed that the human task in the world at present should be one of striving to regain the dominion over the created order that, though lost at the Fall, God still intended humankind to exercise. From this point of view the purpose of natural science is, as T. F. Torrance notes, "to extend the *regnum hominis* over nature."[20] It is this ethical impulse, Torrance contends, that interprets the activistic tenor of modern scientific culture as well as the emergence of the modern understanding of humankind as *homo faber*.[21] The spectacular successes of early-modern scientific explanation— itself a visual metaphor—must surely have seemed to Protestant thinkers to confirm the inherent rightness of their amalgamation of recently reformed theological understanding with the older visually biased philosophical quest.

And so it is that the principal concern of the scientific endeavor has, since the seventeenth-century, been with trying to achieve the clearest possible *point of view*. Achieving such a point of view has required us to construe the world as a field of neutral objects, over and against which we must distance ourselves imaginatively if these objects are to be seen and described accurately and objectively. The modern scientific posture of observation goes some distance toward interpreting our culture's peculiar visual bias as well as the way we commonly employ words and speech. Along this line, Walter Ong, perhaps the preeminent analyst of this development, notes:

It is easy to identify the habitat of this hypervisualism. . . . Its habitat is the mentality fostered by the modern world, that is, the Copernican and even more the Newtonian world, where the cosmos is taken to be essentially something seen. In this world the harmony of the spheres, which was not a metaphorical but an operational concept in the old Aristotelian cosmos, is gone. . . . Newton's and Addison's world, purportedly silent because visually constructed, is the cosmic correlative of the noetic world of "clear and distinct" ideas propounded by Descartes and the Encyclopédistes, where you can test whether anything is possible or not by seeing (the term is significant) whether or not you can imagine it (that is, visualize it).[22]

Ong goes on to list the many visually based words we commonly use to describe the activity of the intellect: *insight, intuition, theory, idea, evidence, species, speculation, suspicion, glimmering, to cast light on, illuminate, elucidate, clear, represent, demonstrate, show, explicate,* etc. "The drive to symbolize intellection and understanding by vision," he continues, "that is, to consider intellection and understanding by analogy with vision . . . corresponds to the drive to objectify knowledge, to make it something which is clearly thing-like, nonsubjective, yielding meaning not in depth but off of surface, meaning which can be spread out, ex-plained."[23] Ong concludes, "The entire philosophy of noetics, including the Platonic idea, Cartesian clarity and distinctiveness, Lockean sensational noetics, the Kantian phenomenon, Hegelian phenomenology, Sartrean opacity, and much else, is inextricably involved with thinking of intellection by analogy with vision."[24] And, of course, this epistemological bias toward visualization has only been intensified by the advent of the computer, for computers enable us to model—and hence, to "see"—previously invisible events and processes of immense complexity. Our proficiency of late in unraveling the human genome, for example, would not have been possible without the aid of digital-imaging technology.

Just as Platonic philosophy sought a language immune to the contingencies of ordinary speech, so modern understanding has been increasingly drawn to the exact language of mathematics. Only mathematics is deemed capable of the degree of precision that science, for example, considers appropriate to the positive description of things. Numbers, it is felt, carry a degree of accuracy and certainty that far surpasses that of mere words. This preference for mathematical language has significantly impacted modern thought. Indeed, it has been suggested that one of the most decisive changes in the character of Western intellectual life over the last several hundred years has been due to the submission of more and more fields of knowledge to the language of mathematics.[25] Steiner notes:

> The sciences and technologies which govern twentieth-century Western civilization have become "modern" and dominant in exact proportion to their mathematical formalization. Larger and larger domains of discovery, of scientific theory, of productive technological appliance have passed out of reach of verbal articulation and of alphabetic notation. . . . Common speech is Ptolemaic, alchemical, opaquely metaphoric in respect of the existential matter of the world as science and engineering perceive it.[26]

It has even been suggested that in the final analysis, all of life must somehow be reducible to a complete and consistent system of logical and mathematical operations.[27] Even those cultural fields and practices that have not yet been entirely surrendered to mathematical formalization have tended to become increasingly abstract and distanced from ordinary life, requiring ever more complicated conceptual apparatuses that are expressible only in highly specialized and technical languages. "At the heart of futurity," Steiner laments, "lies the 'byte' and the number."[28]

All of these cultural developments hinge upon a worldview in which observers imagine themselves to stand outside and above a world of objects, observing how these objects are related to each other spatially and over time and recapitulating these relations either in the exact language of mathematics or at least in terms of abstract theoretical constructs. William Poteat and others have labeled this distinctively modern outlook "Cartesian," not because it necessarily originated in the work of Descartes, but because many of its core assumptions appear to have converged in the explicit philosophical doctrines that Descartes espoused.[29] Cartesian understanding bifurcates reality into a world of material objects, on the one hand, and, on the other, "thinking substances," which somehow transcend this world of objects—a world that includes even our own bodies. While philosophical reflection about language has, since the seventeenth century, suggested that words and speech are where these two aspects of reality somehow overlap, no one has yet managed to explain exactly how they do so. Cartesian understanding has thus left us with a gap that separates "'thinking substance" from the world of objects as well as gaps separating individual "thinking substances" from each other. As Poteat notes:

> Descartes, having officially declared the incommen-surability of extended things and thinking things, was then quite unable to suggest a plausible way in which they might, even so, have some fundamental

connection with one another. No one starting with the same picture of man's relation to nature, to his own body, to time and his own ego, and therefore being constrained by the logic of this picture, has been able to offer, in the three hundred years since Descartes, a more plausible suggestion as to how minds and bodies are to be brought together. During this time hardly any of our debates, explicit or by implication, over the nature of man in the world has failed to move, rather despairingly, back and forth between matter and mind, object and subject, the world as we cannot help fancying it to be, eternally in itself, and the world as it presents itself to us in our perceptions.[30]

While Descartes can hardly be blamed for our present difficulties, it is true that for the last several hundred years we have been encouraged to try to become "the masters and possessors of nature" by means of a cognitive exercise in which we objectify the world and reduce it to mathematical language for the sake of trying to manage it technologically.[31] If the world can only be unified by means of theoretical constructs, and particularly if we can get to the point of being able to *see* things clearly enough to describe them mathematically, so the modern argument runs, then we ought to be able to exert more effective control over our circumstances.

Pictures alone cannot render things intelligible, however, and although visualizing the surface relations between things may well be adequate for certain practical tasks and actions, genuinely personal understanding must be mediated by speech in addition to pictures, and particularly by the words and speech of personal commitment.[32] Yet within the posture of objectivity most of our words will already have become mere indicators and descriptors. Rather than understanding our words and speech to establish a *world* within which it may be possible, by virtue of our having spoken personally and in good faith, to come to a shared understanding, Cartesian logic tends to convert words and speech into observational tools, in effect turning words into pictures. Ong writes:

> What is distinctive of the visualist development leading to our modern technological culture is that it learns to vocalize visual observation far more accurately and elaborately than primitive man, by vocalizing it manages to intellectualize it, and by intellectualizing it comes to generate further specific visual observations, and so on. The visualism we are talking of is thus a visualism strengthened by intimate association with voice, directly in speech or indirectly through script. This association is capital. For if vision is the most tempting symbol for knowing, noetic activity itself is rooted directly or indirectly in the world of sound, through vocalization and hearing. In order to make what we see scientifically usable, we have to be able to verbalize it, and that in elaborately controlled ways. For man there is no understanding without some involvement in words.[33]

We still rely on words, then, and indeed we often find ourselves overwhelmed by concepts, theories, analyses, and information—all of which are expressed in words—but we tend to have a visualist appreciation of these words and therefore of what speaking truthfully means. Instead of understanding words and speech dialogically, that is, as creating the possibility of fellowship and communion on the basis of faithful address and response, we have come to understand words simply as containers of more-or-less accurate information about how the world works and, hopefully, about how it can be made to work for us.

An additional problem with Cartesian understanding is that it is difficult to know just who is doing the observing. Ong cites Bernard Lonergan, for example, as having noticed that a significant consequence of thinking about knowledge and knowing solely through the analogy of vision is that, while objects are revealed in great detail from such a perspective, the subjects making the observations remain largely invisible. "Objects are paraded before spectators," Lonergan writes, "[but] if the spectator wants to know himself, he must get out in the parade and be looked at. There are no subjects anywhere; for being a subject is not being something that is being looked at, it is being the one who is looking."[34] And so we find that persons and personal relations do not easily survive—if indeed they survive at all—the process of objectification. Recalling our initial suggestion that life consists in distancing and relating, the process of objectification may be said to occur wholly on the side of distancing, that is, of standing back away from things and rendering them into objects to be described and analyzed. Yet when this distancing does not take place for the sake of relating as much as it occurs for the sake of mastery, it tends, humanly and personally speaking, to become sterile and lifeless.

Finally, because visualization necessarily abstracts things out of the stream of living history—as, for example, in a photograph—it cannot adequately reckon with the matter of existence, which is inevitably conditioned by time as well as by place. With respect to the former, our ability to distinguish in speech between the past, the present, and the future tenses is what enables us to make sense of our lives, and makes meaning possible for us. We are only able to interpret the past and to project ourselves into the future, furthermore, from the particular place that we happen to inhabit at present. To float above the world and to occupy no particular place within it, as cataloguing entails, is literally to lack the ground for becoming persons.[35] "[W]here the concept 'place' becomes problematic," Poteat argues, "that of 'person' becomes so too."[36] To the extent that our facility in cataloguing things has accustomed us to speak only in the indicative, and from nowhere in particular, we will face difficulties asking, much less answering, questions about the meaning and significance of our own lives.

Of course, the know-how gained by way of Cartesian objectification has been tremendously useful—indeed, so useful that the cataloguing of things has become a kind of habitual cultural posture. Yet here we perhaps need to be reminded that it is possible to become so thoroughly preoccupied with knowing and making things that we lose touch with our particular time and place and forget that our principal task is somehow to begin to know ourselves. Kierkegaard wrote:

> The way of objective reflection makes the subject accidental, and thereby transforms existence into something indifferent, something vanishing. Away from the subject the objective way of reflection leads to the objective truth, and while the subject and his subjectivity become indifferent, the truth also becomes indifferent, and this indifference is precisely its objective validity; for all interest, like all decisiveness, is rooted in subjectivity. The way of objective reflection leads to abstract thought, to mathematics, to historical knowledge of different kinds; and it always leads away from the subject, whose existence or non-existence, and from the objective point of view quite rightly, becomes infinitely indifferent.[37]

This would appear to be true of a good deal of the scientific and technical information surrounding us today.

Mass-mediated Words, Images, and Words as Images

Admittedly, our analysis of the visual bias of modern thought may itself seem rather abstract, but it is important to stress that it has, by now, so infiltrated the popular imagination that it has significantly transformed Western culture. Print technology is at least partly responsible for this transformation, for print, as Ong notes, substitutes the eye for the ear and prioritizes the cognitive importance of sight. Our increasing reliance upon printed materials has led to a fundamental shift in our attitudes toward words. We have come, as Ong writes,

> to react to words less and less as sounds and more and more as *items deployed in space*. Printing made the location of words on a page the same in every copy of a particular edition, giving a text a fixed home in space impossible even to imagine effectively in a pretypological culture. Printing thus heightened the value of the visual imagination and the visual memory and made accessible a diagrammatic approach to knowledge . . . . Typography did more than merely "spread" ideas. It gave urgency to the very metaphor that ideas were items which could be "spread."[38]

Ong goes on to suggest that the "diagrammatic approach to knowledge" was epitomized in an instructional method known as Ramism, named after sixteenth-century educator Peter Ramus. Ramus believed that virtually any kind of knowledge could be effectively and efficiently itemized, diagrammed, and, in effect, packaged such as to be readily assimilated by anyone able to read and purchase printed material. In a sense, Ramus's method was the precursor to the many "how to" manuals that fill the shelves of our bookstores today. His method apparently held a particular appeal for the rising commercial classes in sixteenth- and seventeenth-century Europe, which sought the advantages of formal education, desired to procure such advantages quickly and efficiently, and identified readily with Ramus's "accountant's approach" to knowledge.[39] "A young boy taught the principles of method," Ong notes, "could feel assured in advance of control of any body of knowledge which might come his way. If he were intelligent, he might set out to organize all human knowledge according to some principles of method, confident even before he approached a new field that he would know quite well how to deal with it."[40] Ramus's educational method was well suited to represent the many and varied insights of the "new philosophy" of empirical science, and it commenced an educational trend that would eventually give rise to the grand systems of nineteenth-century thought, in which observers sought to describe, catalogue, and "ex-plain" everything from the origins and evolution of animal species, to the varieties and development of human cultures, to the history of religions, to the systematic unfolding of universal history itself.

Although we no longer possess anything like the analytical confidence of the nineteenth-century and have grown increasingly suspicious of grand theories and systems, we still tend to think of education as a process of arranging, cataloguing, and transmitting information. Indeed, the Ramist ideal corresponds quite closely to what many of the advocates of information technology have promised us most recently—that is, that it soon will be possible for us to organize, catalogue, and retrieve information in such a way that whatever knowledge we need will always be instantly at hand. As an advertisement for

M.C.I. Communications fiber-optic technology put this several years ago: "The space-time continuum is being challenged. The notion of communication is changed forever. All the information in the universe will soon be accessible to everyone at every moment." What are we to make of promises like this? Even allowing for their Madison Avenue rhetoric, it would seem that a great many people today have come to imagine life as a series of problems for which more and more information must somehow provide the solutions. We expect to receive this information, furthermore, in the form of words, images, and words deployed as images in space, increasingly in cyberspace. Recalling our initial parable, we have become largely satisfied simply with assembling and arranging bits of "island news."

Summing up these developments, we might say that for the last several hundred years we have conceived of words and knowledge, in effect, as containers of factual material to be catalogued as needs arise and, most recently, as information to be digitized and broadcast using machine technology. Our cognitive bias toward visualization has led to an explosion of scientific knowledge and to fabulous technical accomplishments. It has enabled us to imagine ourselves observing our world from anywhere and from any perspective, a cognitive skill that has facilitated everything from Einstein's theory of relativity to our recent unraveling of the human genome. Indeed, in spite of assertions that we have entered a postmodern era, modern science and technology continue to surge forward, visualizing more and more aspects of experience. Enhanced by digital processing, we are poised on the threshold of any number of strikingly powerful developments, from genetic engineering, to nanotechnology, to manned missions to Mars. Never has our ability to describe, understand, and control the events and processes of our world been greater.

Yet the contemporary *worldview* continues to be beset by a number of stubborn dualisms, between subjects and objects, between minds and bodies, between our understanding of the way things (including our bodies) work and our understanding of ourselves as persons. Indeed, the rift that has opened up between our technical accomplishments and our self-knowledge appears to be widening rather than narrowing as our knowledge and access to information increases. In part this is because of the sheer impersonality of scientific and technological speech. None of this new knowledge is really addressed to us as persons. Nowhere are we named within it. Indeed, quite often, the language of science and technology is entirely devoid of personal pronouns.[41] Rather it is knowledge *sub species aeternitatis*, knowable in principle by anyone, anywhere, and at any time. Modern science and technology thus present us with a vast catalogue of indications and synthetic propositions concerning events, processes, and dispositions to behavior, but how we are supposed to fit as persons within this vast compendium is never made entirely clear. Indeed, there tends to be a fairly significant discrepancy between our "ex-planations" of human life and our actual experience of it. As Romano Guardini observes:

> No man truly aware of his own human nature will admit that he can discover himself in the theories of modern anthropology—be they biological, psychological, sociological or any other. Only the accidents of man—his attributes, his relations, his forms—make up these theories; they never take man simply as he is. They speak about man, but they never really see man. They approach him, but they never truly find him. They handle him, but they never grip him as he actually is. . . . Mechanical, biological, psychological or sociological abstractions are all variations of a basic

urge to make man one with "nature," even if it be a "nature of the spirit." But a vital reality escapes this type of mind; namely, man's very act of being which constitutes a man in the primitive, absolute sense, which makes man a man at the very core of his self, which makes him a finite person existing. This is what the existing man is even when he does not want to be, even when he denies his own nature.[42]

But our theories appear to lack any kind of appreciation of the contingency of our own speech and actions. Freedom remains invisible to the objective rendering of human events. The so-called human sciences are thus able to observe us acting and to describe our actions in great detail, but they are theoretically bound to reduce our actions to behaviors, and perhaps ultimately to biochemical events and processes. From a scientific perspective nothing genuinely contingent—and therefore genuinely personal—is ever really explicable. Because it is not entirely clear just who is compiling this vast catalogue of knowledge and why, we have grown increasingly confused about what all of this information is for. As Gabriel Marcel commented a number of years ago: "It is as if man, overburdened by the weight of technics, knows less and less where he stands in regard to what matters to him and what doesn't, to what is precious and what is worthless."[43] Finally, because the intention of scientific and technical language is simply to picture the world and describe it,[44] it is poorly suited to address the matter of our existence. To the extent that scientific understanding attempts to interpret dread, anxiety, despair, and other existential realities, it does so only in terms of objective physical and environmental factors or, to put this in the language of our initial parable, only in terms of "island" processes and events. That dread, anxiety, and despair might stem, ultimately, from the fact that we are not actually at home in this present age is rarely, if ever, considered.

Even as we have come to know more and more about a great many things in our world we have become increasingly perplexed about the meaning of our lives and how we ought, therefore, to prepare for death. "Our age," Kierkegaard noted, "is essentially one of understanding and reflection, without passion, momentarily bursting into enthusiasm, and shrewdly relapsing into repose."[45] The repose into which we relapse, furthermore, is—ironically—most often that of activity and busyness, for busyness distracts us from facing the disconcerting realization that more often than not we do not really have any clear idea of who we are and what we are doing.

Of course, the mention of distraction suggests another use to which words have been put in recent times. For although modern know-how may initially have been catalogued in the interests of scientific progress and education, enterprising publishers were quick to realize that a literate public presented an enormous market for words packaged simply to inform and, perhaps even more importantly, to entertain. The subsequent development of technologies designed to convey informative or entertaining words and images has had an extraordinary impact upon contemporary culture. By now, the production and distribution of what has been termed "infotainment" by enormous trans-national corporations accounts for a significant percentage of our entire cultural output.

Yet because the visual bias of the modern *worldview* has prepared us to conceive of words simply as containers of information arranged on a level visual surface, the words and speech of amusement and entertainment lie on essentially the same plane as those of objective science and historical understanding. What this means is that the modern expectation that we would eventually be able to discover who we are by means of empirical science and historical investigation has, by now, been overwhelmed by a veritable avalanche of pseudo-scientific "findings" and even patently bogus "opinions." Indeed it seems that fact and fiction, history and hearsay, truth and falsehood all circulate together with nearly equal authority within contemporary culture. No idea or theory is so absurd as not to qualify for its five minutes on the evening news. No truth is allowed to stand out in such a way as not to be entertainingly deniable. This has resulted in what the late Jacques Ellul termed "the humiliation of the word," a situation in which the power of words to establish us personally in existence, to situate us in a *world* of shared understanding, and to point us in the direction of the truth of things has been all but lost.[46] As words increasingly function as indications only of what seems to be the case at any given moment, it has become more and more difficult to say anything truthful about anything. "Under these circumstances," Ellul laments:

> the word no longer deserves to be believed. This is our present situation. The Word is devaluated in our day because it has come to be used only to express reality [that is, to express what may or may not *appear* to be the case]. Thus no one puts his whole weight behind what he says, and such a word appears useless. Indeed, it is useless, partly because it is a falsehood; it is completely useless because its only true value has been repudiated.[47]

The only true value of words, Ellul believed, is to establish the truth of existence. When our words fail to speak this truth, or when the situation is such that they cannot do so—indeed, when the matter of existence fails even to be of much interest to many people—Ellul believed that our speech must of necessity become decadent and empty.

The peculiar quality of modern journalism is instructive in this connection. By focusing narrowly on the events of each day, journalism makes the world appear as an endless jumble of events through which it is difficult, if not impossible, to discern anything beyond the relatively base motivations of lust, calculated self-interest, and the will to power. Journalism, in short, is not able to impart anything like wisdom. Rather it is only able to report on the surface of things and events. The invention of the journal, or regular periodical, was thus a significant milestone in the development of modern secular consciousness. "Periodical publication suggests a new tempo and urgency in the world's affairs," historian John Sommerville writes, "[b]eing informed replaces the ideal of being wise, and the day or the week becomes the focus of attention, rather than eternity."[48] Journalism's contraction of the temporal horizon to isolated twenty-four-hour periods has contributed quite substantially to the increasingly vacant quality of modern society and culture. By narrowing the compass of meaning only to the news of each day, journalism renders the qualities of character, perseverance, fidelity, and hope increasingly pointless. As Steiner notes:

> The genius of the age is that of journalism. Journalism throngs every rift and cranny of our consciousness. It does so because the press and the media are far more than a technical instrument and commercial enterprise. The root-phenomenology of the journalistic is, in a sense, metaphysical. It articulates an epistemology and ethics of spurious temporality. Journalistic presentation generates a temporality of equivalent instantaneity. All things are more or less

of equal import; all are only daily. Correspondingly, the content, the possible significance of the material which journalism communicates, is "remaindered" the day after. The journalistic vision sharpens to the point of maximum impact every event, every individual and social configuration; but the honing is uniform. Political enormity and the circus, the leaps of science and those of the athlete, apocalypse and indigestion, are given the same edge. Paradoxically, this monotone of graphic urgency anaesthetizes. The utmost beauty or terror are shredded at close of day. We are made whole again, and expectant, in time for the morning edition.[49]

In a way that is perhaps even more bewildering than the super-abundance of scientific and technical information, journalism presents us with vast quantities of disparate indications, descriptions, events, happenings, images, and surface impressions. It overwhelms us with the words and speech of catalogue.

The "spurious temporality" to which Steiner refers reflects the timelessness of the modern visual bias and its tendency to present knowledge and information on an essentially flat visual plane. Yet the quality of "news" today says a number of other things about our culture as well, namely its concupiscence and givenness to sensuality, violence, and *ressentiment*. The willingness with which we consume "news," furthermore, betrays an inordinate desire for distraction. As Aldous Huxley comments in *Brave New World Revisited*:

> [T]he early advocates of . . . a free press envisaged only two possibilities: the propaganda might be true, or it might be false. They did not foresee what in fact has happened, above all in our Western capitalist democracies—the development of a vast mass com-

municated industry, concerned in the main with neither the true nor the false, but with the unreal, the more or less totally irrelevant. In a word, they failed to take into account man's almost infinite appetite for distractions.[50]

The peculiarly irresponsible quality of the "news" also discloses a flight from the deeply humanizing—but serious and difficult—responsibility for owning up to the words that we speak to each other. It is far easier and safer simply to blend in with others and to voice the anonymous opinions of the crowd.

And so we find ourselves deluged, on the one hand, by vast quantities of information and, on the other, by a plethora of opinions. This information and all of these opinions tend to reach our eyes and ears as anonymous words available to us as the anonymous consumers of words. As our means of communication have become more and more technically advanced, that which we actually have to communicate has become less and less personally meaningful. In the midst of these millions of words, almost no one says "I" or speaks to a "you." Kierkegaard characterized early nineteenth-century Denmark as the "golden age of prattle-peddlers."[51] "In a certain sense," he commented, "there is something horrible about contemplating the whole mob of publishers, book-sellers, journalists, authors—all of them working day and night in the service of confusion, because men will not become sober and understand that relatively little knowledge is needed to be truly human."[52] Just imagine what Kierkegaard would have to say about cable television and the world-wide-web!

Even when we decide that we want to say something serious and truthful today, we increasingly find that the words that might once have enabled us to do so have been emptied of meaning and *gravitas*. "Truth," "love," "justice," "freedom"—

even the word "God"—are thrown about these days with little earnestness or seriousness. Our culture has become, as Steiner has lamented, "a wind-tunnel of gossip."[53] "This world," he writes, "will end neither with a bang nor a whimper, but with a headline, a slogan."[54] No small wonder, then, that so many have concluded that language is simply a kind of game and that words simply float on the surface of a restless sea of passion and desire.

Concluding this discussion of catalogue, we note that one of the more profound discoveries with which the modern age may be said to have been inaugurated was the notion that we could, by imagining ourselves as observers standing outside and above the flux of ordinary experience, finally begin to see our world more clearly and objectively, and that in so doing we might manage to take more effective control over our material and social circumstances. It was thought that by envisioning the inherent rationality and intelligibility of the natural order of things, we might eventually be able to discover who we are and how we ought to live. This visual and empirical orientation has, by now, been tremendously fruitful and has given rise to any number of remarkable technical accomplishments. Yet our visual bias has also tended to eclipse another way of understanding the importance of words and speech—always a minority position within Western culture—which suggests that personally uttered words and speech are ultimately what must establish whatever stability and coherence we might expect to enjoy in this world, as well as in the next. Even as it has become increasingly evident of late that the rationality and intelligibility built into the nature of things and revealed by the methods of science does not finally provide answers to the questions of existence, we have not yet been moved as a culture to reconsider this older alternative. Words have been so "humiliated," and we have been so beset by anonymous opinions and impersonal information, that many today are tempted to become cynical, to hold the words of others at arm's length, and perhaps even to withhold their commitment to the words they themselves speak. In a sense, it is as if we have become conscious of being castaway, but have lost hope that news will ever come from "across the sea."

Finally, although one would think that our culture's cynicism would at least leave it less susceptible to exploitation and manipulation, in fact this cynicism leaves us profoundly more vulnerable to false hopes and false promises. As Joseph Pieper cautions in a little book entitled *Abuse of Language, Abuse of Power*, at the moment when public discourse becomes neutralized with respect to matters of truth and existence, it stands ready to be used in the service of the will-to-power.[55] A culture full of the impersonal words and speech of catalogue, in other words, stands ready to be filled also with the words and speech of *monologue*. And so it is to the willful and manipulative use of words and speech that we must turn.

3

Monologue

S EVERAL YEARS AGO, TWO teams of researchers an-
nounced at a press conference that they had completed
the first inventory of the human genome. Although
they emphasized that this remarkable achievement was only
preliminary to understanding how each gene actually func-
tions, the researchers were confident that such knowledge
would be forthcoming and that scientists would soon, on the
basis of increasingly sophisticated genetic analysis, be able to
develop therapies for all sorts of human ailments, including
cancer and perhaps eventually for aging and decrepitude. The
implications of this achievement are immense. Perhaps not
since the development of the first atomic bomb has a technical
capability so clearly underscored the risks and responsibilities of
our rapidly expanding catalogue of knowledge. Of course, we
hope that the know-how revealed by genetic research will only
be used to improve the quality of human life, but we are aware
that the same research must also become available to those who
would construct biological weapons. We suspect, in any event,
that this knowledge will not be—and cannot ever be made to
be—entirely immune to the law of unintended consequences.

The discrepancy between our scientific and technological
proficiency and the impoverished state of our self-knowledge

seemed to be personified in the person of President William Clinton, when he stood beside the researchers at their press conference and likened their achievement to having discovered the "language of God." God, it would seem, is also an engineer who speaks in a language of proteins and statistical probabilities, and learning to speak this language would seem to hold out the promise of godlike power. But will learning to speak the language of proteins and probabilities make those who master it wholly and unambiguously good, as God is? Of course not. Is it likely to make us any wiser, even if it does enhance our technical proficiency? Even if we hope that it will, I suspect that we already know that it will not. After all, why should this particular technological achievement make us any more just or merciful or gracious than all of the other discoveries that we have made in recent times? Instead, this remarkable extension of our already vast catalogue of knowledge into the realm of genetics will probably not ensure much beyond the fact that we will continue down the modern path of imagining the world— and imagining ourselves within it—as engineerable objects. After all, as Peter Berger, a noted theorist of modernity, has observed:

> Modernity means (in intention if not in fact) that men take control over the world and over themselves. What previously was experienced as fate now becomes an arena of choices. In principle, there is the assumption that all human problems can be converted into technical problems, and if the techniques to solve certain problems do not as yet exist, then they will have to be invented. The world becomes ever more 'makeable.'[1]

Yet as we have seen, the assumption that the world is "makeable" and that the primary human task in the world is to make things can obscure our understanding of ourselves as persons as well as our appreciation of our existential predicament as "castaways" in this world. Although genetic sequencing may well be understood as a kind of language, we had better hope that it is not the language of God, for it neither addresses us by name nor illuminates the ground of our existence as persons before God. While it is reasonable to hope that we might find cures for such things as muscular dystrophy and ovarian cancer, we should not expect genetic research to reveal who we really are, and we should not—short of discovering who we really are in some other way—be surprised if this portentous technical know-how is made to serve controversial, if not utterly evil, purposes.

I mention the Human Genome Project here at the outset of our discussion of monologue because willful and manipulative speech appears to propagate especially well within the space that exists between our increasingly vast accumulation of knowledge about the world and our impoverished—or at least underdeveloped—self-understanding. Walker Percy put this rather wickedly at the beginning of *Lost in the Cosmos*: "How is it possible for the man who designed Voyager 19, which arrived at Titania, a satellite of Uranus, three seconds off schedule and a hundred yards off course after a flight of six years, to be one of the most screwed-up creatures in California—or the Cosmos[?]"[2] It is possible, he went on to suggest, because the kind of scientific and technical understanding that enables us to do such remarkable things—the kind of knowledge our culture is almost entirely preoccupied with—is almost completely devoid of any kind of grounding for existential awareness. Indeed, in many ways it seems that the more expert we become at making things the more "screwed-up" we actually get.

Yet the combination of technical prowess and inadequate self-understanding is no laughing matter. For it presents a dangerous situation in which the technical will-to-power is rather easily—indeed *eagerly*—mistaken for wisdom. Nietzsche's comment, cited by Max Weber at the end of *The Protestant Ethic and the Spirit of Capitalism*, is apposite: "Specialists without spirit, sensualists without heart; this nullity imagines that it has attained a level of civilization never before achieved."[3] Along this line, I remember someone suggesting when I was heading off to university for the first time that I would soon be exposed to the most comprehensive understanding of the world that any generation had ever attained. The comment filled me with anticipation and pride, and while I did not actually find it to be true, I did find many who believe that it is. Arnold Gehlen, in *Man in the Age of Technology*, characterized the social psychology of the modern age as *pleonexia*, an oddly powerful combination of greed, arrogance, and ambition, all of which tend in the direction of recklessness and blind us to our acute need for self-examination.

It should not come as any great surprise, then, to find that our greed, arrogance, and ambition have found their primary expression in speech, and that the powerful catalogue of information we have assembled over the course of the last several hundred years has tempted us to use words and speech willfully and manipulatively. Having striven to become "the masters and possessors of nature" and having, by now, become technically proficient beyond the wildest dreams of Descartes, we have also become increasingly willful and manipulative in our use of words. The eclipse of the personalizing speech of dialogue by the impersonal speech of catalogue has inevitably given rise to the depersonalizing speech of monologue.

Derived from the Greek words *mono* (one) and *logos* (word), monologue simply means "one speaker" or "to speak alone." Webster's Dictionary defines monologue as "a dramatic sketch performed by one actor" speaking, as it were, to him- or herself. Webster's goes on to define monologue as "a long speech monopolizing conversation," a speech in which conversation is effectively rendered moot by the self-absorbed and overbearing disposition of one speaker. I will use the word "monologue" in the following discussion in this sense, where monologue will denote a posture of willfulness, where there is really only one speaker and one active voice, and where others are acknowledged only as occasions for hearing that one active voice speak. In monologue the speaker has an unbounded sense of him- or herself, seeking from others only that which somehow confirms his or her own desires.[4] Monological words, furthermore, are used only as means to an end, most often to the end of control. Speaking out of a posture of monologue, then, does not simply monopolize the conversation; rather it destroys any possibility of conversation. As the possibility of conversation is destroyed, so is the possibility of personalizing speech. Monologue is therefore not simply impersonal speech, but it is actively depersonalizing.

And so we find that contemporary culture is full not only of the impersonal speech of catalogue but also of the willful and depersonalizing speech of monologue. We see this in the political realm, with the use of propaganda and ideological assertion. We see this in the technical realm, where the specialized vocabularies of catalogue are employed to evade responsibility and to overwhelm those who would object to technical developments in the name of ethics. We see it in the realm of commerce, where words and speech are painstakingly crafted not to communicate but rather to influence consumers and to "brand" proprietary products and services. We see it also in the cynical use of irony and equivocation for the sake of the confusion they generate, behind which power is often consolidated. How often do we discover too late that an individual's or an organization's real intentions have, in effect, been attached as riders to attractive propositions expressly designed to hide those intentions? How often do we find that we need professional legal assistance simply to ferret out all of the falsehoods written into ordinary communications and transactions? How often do we feel that we are being "talked down to" or "talked at" and not really addressed by those in positions of power? If we find these sorts of things increasingly distressing today, this is due to the prevalence of monological speech in contemporary culture. Rather than enabling us to come at a shared understanding as *we*, monologue strives to create the conditions in which it is possible for a speaker to say, as Lewis Carroll writes in *Alice in Wonderland*, "words mean what *I* want them to mean, no more and no less."

In the little book mentioned at the end of the last chapter, *Abuse of Language, Abuse of Power*, Joseph Pieper discusses the manipulative use of language under the heading of "sophistry," the art of using words and speech to justify one's own social position and/or exercise of power. Pieper frames this discussion by reviewing Plato's lifelong battle with the Sophists, "those highly paid and popularly applauded experts in the art of twisting words, who were able to sweet-talk something bad into something good and to turn white into black."³ Pieper observes that Plato places the Sophists in opposition to Socrates in his *Dialogues*, and although Plato depicts them as learned—even attractive—their clever verbal constructions are revealed in the ensuing dialogue to obscure truth. Their aspirations, furthermore, are revealed to extend no further than the legitimation of their privileged social position.

Of course, the duplicitous legitimation of privilege is reprehensible in itself, yet Pieper notes that Plato's chief criticism of the Sophists was not that their sophisticated abuse of language often masked arrogance and ambition, but that their clever constructions subverted the meanings of words, making it all the more difficult for those of good will to offer rational and intelligible resistance to further abuse. Once the word "justice" has been effectively used to legitimate a particular social interest, for example, it becomes problematic to challenge this social interest in the name of justice. Once the word "democratic" has been successfully attached to a particular platform, it becomes difficult to criticize this platform in the name of democracy. Contemporary political life provides any number of examples of this process. Consider the notion of "social justice," which by now has been used by so many disparate groups to justify so many disparate social and political interests that it has become all but useless as an ethical idea. The use of the word "right" is instructive in this connection as well. The word has been attached to so many different and often competing social and political interests—"civil *rights*," "human *rights*," "women's' *rights*," "the *rights* of the unborn"— that it has become increasingly difficult to employ the notion of "right" in trying to decide between conflicting groups and proposals. In Plato's mind, then, the problem with sophistry is that it confuses and ultimately corrupts language. At the hands of the Sophists, words and speech were rendered increasingly incapable of sustaining genuine debate and dialogue, and they had become increasingly tainted for use in attempting to disclose the truth of things.

The temptation to use words to legitimate particular social interests is a perennial temptation of the educated, for a good deal of the educational process involves learning how to use words to present one's ideas persuasively and convincingly. Given the emphasis we place upon education today, and given the distinctively modern propensity for naming to overwhelm telling, Pieper contends that the present age has become the age of sophistry *par excellence.*[6] Ours is a culture in which practically anything can be—and probably has been—defended and justified in public speech. One need only to search hard enough for reasons that can be presented in a convincing and persuasive manner. Another name for sophisticated persuasion, Pieper suggests, is *flattery.*

> Flattery here does not mean saying what the other likes to hear, telling him something nice, something to tickle his vanity. And what is thus said is not necessarily a lie. . . . The decisive element is this: having an ulterior motive. I address the other not simply to please him or to tell him something that is true. Rather what I say to him is designed to *get* something from him! This underlying design makes the message a flattery, even in the popular meaning of the word. The other, whom I try to influence with what he likes to hear, ceases to be my partner; he is no longer a fellow subject. Rather he has become for me an object to be manipulated, possibly to be dominated, to be handled and controlled.[7]

Pieper goes on to observe that flattery does not succeed simply on the basis of power and domination, but because those who are flattered allow themselves to be manipulated by accepting the flattering descriptions of themselves proffered by those who would influence them. Flattery, in short, is a two-way street. It is a kind of game in which those who want to wield influence secure the permission—even if only tacitly—of those they seek to influence. This is why successful flattery cannot be too obsequious, but must enable those who are being flattered to deceive themselves about themselves. In this connection Pieper recalls the old churchly saying, *mundus vult decipi* ("The world wants to be deceived"), but adds that the world insists upon being deceived in such a way as to remain in good conscience, which is to say, it must not be made to concede that the flattering descriptions of it are completely disconnected from the truth.[8] Successful flattery must be at least entertainably true, and so sophistry tends to proceed, by and large, on the basis of *half*-truths and rarely on the strength of lies *per se*. For this reason sophistry can be described as a kind of art, and it is often not easily recognizable as sophistry, for a good part of sophistry's artfulness lies in remaining concealed and disguised. Pieper writes:

> It is, therefore, extremely difficult, at times impossible, to take a specific item (such as a novel, a stage play, a movie, a radio commentary, or a critical essay) and identify the borderline that separates genuine communication rooted in reality from the mere manipulation of words aimed solely to impress. Formal excellence alone cannot be the decisive criterion. . . . Yes, even philosophy, theology, and the humanities, just like any fictional literature, however demanding and challenging, in essence may well be mere entertainment in our specific sense here—that is, a form of flattery, extremely refined perhaps, yet nevertheless courting favor to win success. And success in this does not necessarily mean huge sales and large profits. Any form of approval will do.[9]

Pieper's overriding concern is that sophisticated flattery can become so pervasive within a culture that genuine discourse becomes all but impossible. "[W]herever the main purpose of speech is flattery," he writes, "there the word becomes corrupted, and necessarily so. And instead of genuine communication, there will exist something for which *domination* is too benign a term; and more appropriately we should speak of tyranny, of despotism."[10] He writes:

> The very moment . . . that someone in full awareness employs words yet explicitly disregards reality [that is, is not committed to seeking out the truth of things], he in fact ceases to communicate anything to the other. . . . Whoever speaks to another person—not simply, we presume, in spontaneous conversation but using well-considered words, and whoever in so doing is explicitly not committed to the truth—whoever, in other words, is in this guided by something other than the truth—such a person, from that moment on, no longer considers the other as partner, as equal. In fact, he no longer respects the other as a human person. From that moment on, to be precise, all conversation ceases; all dialogue and all communication come to an end.[11]

The vast quantity of jargon-laden scientific and technological information that we have produced in recent times is obviously ripe for sophisticated abuse, and our susceptibility to sophisticated manipulation has been immeasurably increased by the eagerness with which we consume the images and opinions produced by mass media. Indeed, the consolidation of all this information and entertainment into "infotainment" suggests that our culture is one in which, as Pieper notes, "the place of authentic reality is taken over by a fictitious reality;

[our] perception is indeed still directed toward an object, but now it is a *pseudoreality*, deceptively appearing as being real, so much so that it becomes almost impossible any more to discern the truth."[12] Today, Pieper concludes, we need to take very seriously Plato's concern that sophistry can, if left unchecked, leave language incapable of inquiring after the truth of things and hence of sustaining genuine dialogue.

Perhaps the clearest example of manipulative communication today is advertising, which is nearly everywhere we look. "The world may have been 'charged with the grandeur of God' for earlier generations," James Twitchell observes in an interesting study entitled *Adcult USA: The Triumph of Advertising in American Culture*, "but for us it is chock full of paid messages .... Almost every physical object now carries advertising, almost every human environment is suffused with advertising, almost every moment of time is calibrated by advertising."[13] What advertising wants to get from us, of course, is our business, which is to say, our money. The purpose of an advertisement is to attract our attention and subsequently, by way of repetitive suggestion, to move us to desire and eventually to purchase a particular brand of product. As the subtitle of Twitchell's study suggests, advertising has, in effect, become what a good deal of North American culture is all about. Of the thousands of words that reach our eyes and ears each day, a significant and growing percentage of them are commercial.

While the "triumph of advertising" is often interpreted as—and may ultimately turn out to be—a sinister development, it is also helpfully understood as a reflection of the willingness with which we consume words and images as entertainment, something modern corporations are only too happy to sponsor in the interest of selling us the products they make. If we are manipulated by corporations and advertisers, then, this is only because we tacitly given them our permission to do so. After all, advertising is amusing and we know—or at least suppose—that we retain control of our wallets at the point of sale. Advertising has thus become an integral aspect of popular culture, which may be defined as the management and mass-mediation of popular entertainment for profit. From newspapers, to radio broadcasts, to television, to the world wide web, "pop" has become a central aspect of twenty-first-century culture, crossing all lines of genre, nationality, media, and taste.[14] While the high culture of university arts departments and museums may once have been readily distinguishable from folk amusements, distinctions between the two have been increasingly collapsed into the mass-mediated images and narratives of popular culture, with advertising implicated in virtually every step of the process. As Twitchell observes:

> Modern advertising's overwhelming mandate to at-tract attention has made it invade provinces hitherto off-limits to commercialism. In so doing Adcult has collapsed these often contentious cultures [i.e., "high" versus "folk"] into a monolithic, worldwide order immediately recognized by the House of Windsor and the tribe of Zulu. From high culture to folk, from high brow to low, from Aesthetica to Vulgaria, commercial speech is not so much shouting down competing voices as enlisting them to sing the same tune. If ever there is to be global village, it will be because the town crier works in advertising.[15]

Of course, contemporary consumer behavior and "adcult" may be said to disclose the archetypically modern decision to set the philosophical and theological pursuit of truth off to one side for the sake of the comfort and convenience made possible by scientific, technological, and commercial development.[16]

From this perspective advertising simply reiterates a core modern belief, i.e., that we can, in effect, construct happiness on the basis of secular pragmatism. We will return to this point in a moment. At present it is important simply to notice that the various enterprises that form "adcult" share a common orientation toward words and speech, an orientation not far removed from Pieper's notion of *flattery*. Here words and speech are not used to communicate *per se* but to influence, to move the listener or viewer to act in accordance with the speaker's— or rather producer's—designs and desires. The object of commercial speech is not to arrive at a shared understanding on the basis of our common search for truth so much as it is simply to encourage us to believe that the quality of our lives will somehow be enhanced through continued—indeed, continuous—consumption.

The machinery of "adcult" has also been employed for political purposes in modern democratic culture. From the "Eisenhower Answers America" campaign of 1952 to today's seemingly endless electioneering, electoral politics has increasingly become a matter of expensive and carefully crafted sophistry. As Dan Nimmo notes in a study entitled *The Political Persuaders: The Techniques of Modern Election Campaigns*,

> What each citizen derives from the mass media in a political campaign is not information . . . but entertainment. . . . Alone as a member of a mass audience his senses are titillated and temporarily gratified. He does not internalize what he perceives in the sense that his attitudes are changed, but he remembers and forgets in the rote fashion of learning without involvement. In the process he comes to a vote decision congenial to his perceptions. The convergence of these individual decisions on election day constitutes

the ultimate measure of the effectiveness of the mediated campaign.[17]

A successful political campaign today, in other words, links a candidate to those opinions already held by a large number—hopefully a majority—of voters. The object of the campaign is not to educate or to elucidate, and neither is it to engage in any kind of reasoned discourse. Rather it is simply to suggest to voters that a vote for Candidate X is congenial to their concerns and interests and, conversely, that a vote for the opposing candidate will somehow threaten these same concerns and interests. "If people see in an object what they project into it," Nimmo observes, "image candidates must be sufficiently flexible receptacles to satisfy a wide variety of image predispositions."[18] He concludes: "Without question the new technology introduces not only the possibility but indeed the likelihood of systematic deception in electoral politics."[19]

It would be mistaken to blame advertisers and business corporations for this development, however. Contemporary political life simply betrays the same bias toward the pragmatic and technical that we discussed in the last chapter under the heading of Cartesianism. For the last several centuries, we have been encouraged to believe that political community can be built, in effect, from scratch on the basis of newly discovered scientific and technical information. Implicit in the modern political discourse is a willingness to take an engineering approach to social and political realities, which inevitably leads to the use of words and speech as means to political ends, ends that apparently justify such means.

Furthermore, because modern politics is principally concerned with the secular realm, political discourse tends to focus on the immediate gratification of the material desires of the electorate. As political philosopher Michael Oakeshott noted a

number of years ago in a series of provocative essays entitled
Rationalism and Politics:

> The politics [that Cartesian rationalism] inspires may
> be called the politics of felt need; for the Rationalist,
> politics are always charged with the feeling of the
> moment. He waits upon circumstance to provide him
> with his problems, but rejects its aid in their solution.
> That anything should be allowed to stand between a
> society and the satisfaction of the felt needs of each
> moment in its history must appear to the Rationalist
> a piece of mysticism and nonsense. . . . Thus, poli-
> tical life is resolved into a succession of crises, each
> to be surmounted by the application of "reason"
> [technique].[20]

Political solutions to this succession of crises are communicated,
furthermore, by way of ideological narratives that—precisely
because they purport to comprehend and "ex-plain" the
world—promise power over the world and legitimate the use
of this power. The two most salient features of these political
narratives are their promise of control[21] and their capacity for
mobilizing mass support for political action.[22] This explains
why ideologies are commonly comprehensive and yet also
readily communicable, for even as they purport to redress
a myriad of complex social problems, they must be relatively
easy to understand if they are to be effective in mobilizing mass
support. As Arnold Gehlen observes:

> One can also detect a tendency to take up crystallized,
> simplified, dogmatized systems of thought, each
> capable, for all their differences, of providing their
> supporters with preconstituted positions upon all moral
> and philosophical questions. Complex and sophist-

icated sets of ethical or intellectual issues become
politicized and stereotyped. On the one hand this has
the facilitating effect of yielding simpler orderings; on
the other it induces a narrowing and contracting of
the horizons of thought. . . . A reality that is infinitely
complex, many-sided, and changeable is thus made
artificially simple and graspable so as to bring about
the proximity indispensable to all morality.[23]

The specific skills of advertisers come into play at just this point,
for they effectively and attractively produce and broadcast these
"crystallized, simplified, dogmatized systems of thought." It
is a short step, in other words, from a politics of felt need to
the Madison Avenue sloganeering that contemporary political
pundits decry even as they thrive upon and publicize it.

Yet the "triumph of advertising" in political life has not met
with a great deal of principled resistance, because the language
of traditional ethics no longer seems to apply to contemporary
social and political problems. Rather these problems frequently
appear—largely because of the language used to mediate
them—to be technical problems calling for technical solutions.
Voters are told that what they need is not wisdom as much
as more effective political management. This has led to the
emergence of what Oakeshott terms "the new art of politics":

> the art, not of "ruling" (that is, of seeking the most
> practicable adjustments for the collisions of "indi-
> viduals"), nor even of maintaining the support of a
> majority of individuals in a "parliamentary" assembly,
> but of knowing what offer will collect the most votes
> and making it in such a manner that it appears to come
> from "the people"; the art, in short, of "leading" in the
> modern idiom. Moreover, it is known in advance what
> offer will collect the most votes: the character of the

"mass man" is such that he will be moved only by the
offer of release from the burden of making choices
for himself, the offer of "salvation." And anyone who
makes this offer may confidently demand unlimited
power; it will be given him.[24]

As the horizon of salvation has increasingly been fore-
shortened to this age and to the secular concerns of comfort,
safety, and convenience, voters seem prepared to surrender
themselves to whomever they feel stands the best chance of
satisfying—or at least of not threatening—their more or less
immediately felt needs.

Alexis de Tocqueville was among the first to suggest that
there might be a correlation between democracy in practice
and the increasingly shallow quality of modern culture. Indeed,
one of his principal concerns in *Democracy in America* was that
the increasingly trivial quality of nineteenth-century American
culture might actually be a kind of unintended by-product of
the democratic guarantees of liberty and equality.[25] Basically,
Tocqueville observed that classical liberalism had the effect of
liberating the citizens of liberal democracy from traditional
sources of moral authority which, in effect, left the matters of
goodness and rectitude largely up to each individual to decide
for him- or herself. Democracy had declared its citizens to be
equal, in other words, but in the process had inadvertently
disconnected them from traditional notions of moral order. It
left them free, but oddly alone and self-determining. Yet while
the democratic habit of self-reliance created a national character
that was extraordinarily practical and inventive, it also had
the effect of narrowing the cultural focus to practicality and
invention. "Most of the people in these [democratic] nations,"
Tocqueville wrote,

are extremely eager in the pursuit of immediate
material pleasures and are always discontented with
the position they occupy and always free to leave it.
They think about nothing but ways of changing
their lot and bettering it. For people in this frame of
mind every new way of getting wealth more quickly,
every machine which lessens work, every means of
diminishing the costs of production, every invention
which makes pleasures easier or greater, seems the most
magnificent accomplishment of the human mind.[26]

Success in the realm of the practical, Toqueville contended however, had apparently encouraged nineteenth-century Americans
to imagine that everything in the world must somehow be
explicable in merely technical-rational terms. "Hence," he
wrote, "they have little faith in anything extraordinary and an
almost invincible distaste for the supernatural."[27]

Imagining that everything in the world is explicable in
technical-rational terms inevitably leads people to place a great
deal of emphasis upon the practical efficacy of power. It is hardly
surprising, then, that North American society would eventually
come to be describable in terms of pleonexia. Neither is it
surprising that North American politicians would increasingly
resort to systematic flattery, manipulation, and willfulness—in
short, to monologue—in an attempt to govern such a society.
Basically, monologue is to speech what the machine is to raw
nature, that is, a practical, efficient, and effective way to get a
particular job done. In the case of modern democratic politics,
the job is that of establishing whatever legitimacy is necessary
to secure and exercise political power. "In our time," George
Orwell observes in his celebrated essay "Politics and the English
Language":

political speech and writing are largely the defense of the indefensible. . . . Political language—and with variations this is true of all political parties, from Conservatives to Anarchists—is designed to make lies sound truthful and murder respectable, and to give an appearance of solidity to pure wind.[28]

Or, as George Steiner laments more recently:

In our time, the language of politics has become infested with obscurity and madness. No lie is too gross for strenuous expression, no cruelty too abject to find apologia in the verbiage of historicism. Unless we can restore to the words in our newspapers, laws, and political acts some measure of clarity and stringency of meaning, our lives will draw yet nearer to chaos.[29]

We are flooded today not simply by the impersonal speech of catalogue, but also by the willful and manipulative words and speech of monologue. We may be tempted to think that all of this manipulative speech is more or less harmless, for we know that the advertisers are just trying to sell us things, that campaign promises are never to be taken at face value, etc. Monologue is far from harmless, however. As Pieper observes, following Plato, once the well of language has been poisoned, it becomes impossible for *anyone* to drink from it for *any* purpose. He writes:

[P]recisely this is one of the lessons recognized by Plato through his own experience with the sophists of his time. . . . This lesson, in a nutshell, says: the abuse of political power is fundamentally connected with the sophistic abuse of the word, indeed, finds in it the fertile soil in which to hide and grow and get ready, so much so that the latent potential of the totalitarian poison can be ascertained, as it were, by observing the symptom of the public abuse of language. . . . [T]his Platonic nightmare, I hold, possesses an alarming contemporary relevance. For the general public is being reduced to a state where people not only are unable to find out about the truth but also become unable even to *search* for the truth because they are satisfied with deception and trickery that have determined their convictions, satisfied with a fictitious reality created by design through the abuse of language. This, says Plato, is the worst thing that the sophists are capable of wreaking upon mankind by their corruption of the word.[30]

The abuse of language today is so egregious and obvious—at least once we begin to consider it in light of the requirements of genuine dialogue—that adding to the examples above runs the risk of simply contributing grist to the mill of cynicism and despair. Still, I believe it is important to at least try to fit this abuse into a larger interpretive context, so that we can ponder why we have not resisted it more vigorously, and we can consider how we might go about reviving the personalizing speech of dialogue. This last task I want to reserve for our final chapter, but I want to conclude this discussion of monologue by reviewing several additional interpretations that have been offered for the willful manipulative quality of so many of the words that reach our eyes and ears today.

One interpretation of our predominantly instrumentalist attitude toward words and speech is that it reflects the logic inherent in certain technologies of communication. McLuhan, for example, suggests that the West's pragmatic approach to language stems simply from the practical bias of alphabetic writing and, eventually, of typography. McLuhan writes in *Understanding Media*:

> Only alphabetic cultures have ever mastered connected
> lineal sequences as pervasive forms of psychic and
> social organization. The breaking up of experience
> into uniform units in order to produce faster action
> and change of form (applied knowledge) has been
> the secret of Western power over man and nature
> alike. That is the reason why our Western industrial
> programs have quite involuntarily been so militant,
> and our military programs have been so industrial.
> Both are shaped by the alphabet in their technique of
> transformation and control by making all situations
> uniform and continuous.[31]

To the extent that we have come to see words and speech as tools to be used in the service of largely practical ends, in other words, this is simply because alphabetic writing so readily lends itself to—and indeed encourages—pragmatic thought and action. Yet while McLuhan's celebrated contention that "the medium is the message" is provocative and insightful, it is also reductionistic. Amid his concerns to link cultural developments to particular communications technologies, McLuhan does not pay enough attention to the philosophical and theological commitments that have, as we have seen, narrowed our cultural focus to the practical-rational mastery of nature. To say that Western industrial culture is "involuntarily" militant simply does not do justice to the fact that industrial development has been forcefully *advocated* over the last several hundred years, often in the face of significant opposition.

More helpful, it seems to me, are several suggestions that Jacques Ellul makes in *The Humiliation of the Word*. Ellul believes that the willful abuse of words and speech today is largely explicable in terms of the social interests of two groups that have been placed in charge of cataloguing the world in recent centuries, namely *technicians* and *intellectuals*.[32] Technicians, because their interests lie in getting things done for those that pay them, tend to place a high value upon the efficiency and effectiveness of communication. Indeed, they would reduce language to the unequivocal simplicity of algebra if this were possible. While technicians are not perhaps finally responsible for such things as propaganda, they are almost always the ones who produce and transmit it. Intellectuals, on the other hand, whose claims to authority are attached to their skill at interpreting events and processes, have a clear interest in understanding language as a social construction. Such an understanding shifts attention away from traditional wisdom—now held to be naive—toward the increasingly sophisticated interpretation deemed necessary for understanding the real meaning of things, meaning that is hidden from common sense and ordinary observation. The neo-Marxian understanding of so-called "late-capitalism," for example, a paradigm that survives today almost exclusively in academic enclaves, requires cognitively privileged intellectuals to interpret the meaning of the historical process for the rest of us, who are simply too deeply immersed in it to understand it.

Yet here again the specific social interests of technicians and intellectuals can also be said to reflect the broader philosophical program of modernity, which from the outset has been animated by the desire to take control of things. Whereas traditional wisdom stressed knowing a thing for the sake of admiring and living with it, the modern interest is not so much in the thing itself but rather in what kind of work a thing can be made to do. Romano Guardini writes:

This [modern] knowledge does not inspect; it analyzes. It does not construct a picture of the world, but a formula. Its desire is to achieve power so as to bring force to bear on things, a law that can be formulated rationally. Here we have the basis and character of its dominion: compulsion, arbitrary compulsion devoid of all respect. . . . The new desire for mastery does not in any sense follow natural courses or observe natural proportions. Indeed, it treats these with complete indifference. The new mastery posits its aims arbitrarily on rational grounds.[33]

That this "new mastery" would issue forth in willful and manipulative speech was perhaps inevitable.

It was probably also inevitable that the characteristically modern emphasis upon control would eventually boil down to control of some at the expense of others. "[T]he power of Man to make himself what he pleases means . . . the power of some men to make other men what *they* please," as C. S. Lewis trenchantly observed in *The Abolition of Man*.[34] British philosopher John Macmurray provides a useful schematic history of this peculiar problem.[35] Macmurray notes that it was first recognized toward the end of the Middle Ages that rational social progress was going to require the control of nature, and it was not long thereafter that the "*novum organum*" of the early modern scientific method emerged as the solution to this problem. Yet it became apparent over the course of several successive generations that rational social progress could not really be made until society was itself rationally organized for the sake of such progress. The scientific method thus began to be applied to human behavior in addition to nature as such, individually by way of modern psychology and collectively by means of sociology. Yet this incursion of the methods of science into human affairs gave rise to a number of perplexing questions, which we as a culture have yet to answer. Macmurray continues:

> To control his environment man must control him-
> self, and to control himself he must know how he
> is made and how, in fact, he does behave. But if he
> knows how he behaves, how can that help him to
> behave differently? If he can behave differently, the
> psychology which enables him to do so cannot be a
> true and complete account of how he behaves. If he
> cannot behave differently, what use is his psychology
> to him, and how indeed could he behave so differently
> as to produce it? So far from solving the problem with
> which science began, "How can we control the world?",
> its completion in psychology merely sets the question,
> "Who is to control whom?", and introduces a universal
> struggle to control one another which, if it develops,
> must make all effort to control the environment
> impossible and make the work of science itself equally
> impossible.[36]

Macmurray's mention here of the "universal struggle to control one another" goes some distance toward explaining why so many modern—and now purportedly postmodern—philosophers have been tempted to describe human existence exclusively in terms of the will to power.[37] For while struggle and bloody conflict have characterized the human condition since Cain murdered Abel, a ceaseless struggle for control seems quite literally built into modern societies by reason of the modern quest for technological mastery.

Unfortunately, many of the protests that are today being leveled against the manipulative spirit of modernity serve—albeit ironically—to reinforce and even to amplify the modern tendency to use words and speech willfully. Such would appear to be the case with a good deal of postmodernist thought. At one level, postmodernism may be said to be simply an indictment—similar to that developed in the last chapter—of the impersonal and depersonalizing trajectory of modern scientific and technological development. To the extent that the modern project was launched with the conviction that human reason could—once liberated from ignorance, superstition, and tradition—illuminate the true order of things for the sake of taking control of them, postmodern thinkers have raised the awkward questions of just who is to be allowed to exercise this privilege and for what purposes. Why, the protesters want to know, does it always seem to be the case that the same people—usually white men—get to decide what counts as "truth"? And why are these same people consistently permitted to determine how this "truth" is to be put to work? Such eminently reasonable questions have been raised in order to defend the subjectivity, which is to say the status as subjects, of those—the colonized, persons of color, women, etc.—who have often been treated as mere objects within the modernist purview. In this respect postmodernism may be understood simply as a vote of no confidence in those who have hitherto been allowed to decide what counts as "progress."

Yet postmodern criticism extends beyond simply raising questions about who has been allowed to say just how the various truths revealed by modern methods are to be used, and for whose benefit, to the notion of "truth" itself. Indeed, modernity's commitment to the notion of truth, postmodern critics have asserted, accounts precisely for its repressive tendencies. The conviction that there is such a thing as "truth," critics contend, betrays the assumption that there actually is an underlying order of things and that the coherence and consistency of this order is somehow underwritten by the presence of something that—or, more importantly, of *Someone who*—transcends this order. Such an assumption, they continue, inevitably gives rise to an understanding of the world within which virtue is understood in terms of fitting into "the nature of things," and such an understanding must inevitably translate into authoritarian social practices. What modernists fail to appreciate, the critics continue, is that what really lies underneath the surface of things is not order—indeed, not even ordered change—but rather *dis*order and *alterity*. Critics argue that the fact that the alterity at the heart of things has not generally been recognized and the extent to which our world appears to be ordered and stable are simply optical illusions that stem from the visual bias of the Western philosophical imagination. This is why postmodern critics confess "incredulity with respect to metanarratives."[38] They have grown profoundly suspicious of all systems of thought—whether philosophical or theological—that have ultimate recourse to some transcendent principle of order. All such systems are deemed repressive of human freedom and autonomy.

Such thoroughgoing skepticism has any number of radical implications and calls much of Western civilization into question. Those concerned with defending Western culture in the face of such radical criticism have understandably tended to focus on the threat that postmodern understanding poses to the notion of truth, but the more immediately threatening consequences of postmodern incredulity have to do with its radical understanding of the prospects for words and speech. On the one hand, postmodern critics vigorously advocate for a return to discourse, that is, for a recovery of the primacy of speaking and listening over and against the modern preoccupation with seeing. Yet the critics refuse to permit such a recovery to imply any assumption of *presence*; that is, any assumption of an underlying order of things. The conviction, for example, that it is possible for words and speech to accurately and truthfully refer to things in our experience is repudiated by postmodern critics, as is the belief that meaning can be determinate. Instead, postmodern theorists contend that there can be no meaning in any absolute sense because there is no absolute author. Rather, there is only a multiplicity of "authors" and a throng of "interpreters" that includes, finally, each one of us. Because each of our points of view is so severely limited by our individual circumstances, and because we are so often in competition with one another for scarce resources, we each, in effect, construct meanings that may make sense to us at a given time and place. Yet our constructions are ultimately groundless. They merely float on the surface of a roiling sea of circumstance and desire. Postmodern critics readily admit that such a position is disorienting and disquieting, but they are quick to add that it is also profoundly liberating, for it means that virtually anything that anyone has to say—as long they do not presume to speak the truth—is as valid as anything else.

Granted, a good deal of so-called postmodern sentiment simply reflects reasonable apprehension about ongoing technological and industrial development. Yet the conceptual underpinnings of postmodernist theory are radical and ultimately *theological*. Indeed, the postmodernist theoretical protest stems from a kind of *anti*-theology, which is to say, a refusal—in the name of immanence and egalitarianism—to allow any principle or authority to ground, and therefore to discipline, the use of words and speech. Along this line, Steiner observes that postmodernism's basic insight is that

> the origin of the axiom of meaning and of the God-concept is a shared one. The semantic sign, where it

is held to be meaningful, and divinity "have the same place and time of birth" (Derrida). They constitute the Hebraic-Hellenic copula on which our *Logos*-history and practice have been founded. . . . It is Derrida's strength to have seen so plainly that the issue is neither linguistic-aesthetic nor philosophical in any traditional, debatable sense—where such tradition and debate incorporate, perpetuate the very ghosts which are to be exorcised. The issue is, quite simply, that the meaning of meaning as it is re-insured by the postulate of the existence of God. "In the beginning was the Word." There was no such beginning, says deconstruction; only the play of sounds and markers amid the mutations of time.[39]

A consequence of postmodernism's repudiation of theology is that there can no longer be any stable and potentially ascertainable meaning of meaning; neither can there be any stable notion of personality. "Where the theologically and metaphysically posited principle of a continuous individuality, of a cognitively coherent and ethically responsible ego is dissolved . . . ," Steiner continues, "there can be neither Kant's 'subjective universality,' nor that belief in shared truth-seeking which, from Plato to the present, from the *Phaedrus* to now, had underwritten the ideals of religion, of humanism and of communication."[40] Postmodernist theory, in short, hinges almost entirely upon the presumption that "God is dead."

The roots of such radical ideas reach back into the seventeenth and eighteenth centuries to the purportedly enlightened repudiation of the traditional belief in the possibility of divine revelation. Postmodernist theory also reflects Romanticism's emphasis upon expressive individuality and the impatient Romantic longing to be liberated from traditional social and religious constraints. Yet its critical formative period, as Steiner notes, occurred toward the end of the nineteenth century when a number of poets, authors, and scholars finally began to vent their frustration with the theological affirmations and metaphors implicit in ordinary language. All such affirmation seemed to them, in the light of modern historical criticism, to be both vacuous and hypocritical. Out of such frustration there emerged the suspicion that there is not, finally, any connection at all between the words we use to describe the world and the world itself, suspicion that subsequently led, as Steiner puts it, to a kind of *"break of the covenant between word and world."*[41] This, he believes, was one of the very few genuine revolutions of spirit in Western history.[42]

Yet if, as skeptical theorists had begun to suggest, traditional theological affirmations of the *Word* were no longer able to underwrite the truthfulness of speech, philosophers in the analytic tradition hoped that the structure of language itself might provide insights into the mechanics and constants of human cognition and that logical consistency might at least be substituted for truthfulness in our understanding of language. Indeed, it was thought that it might eventually be possible to so rid ordinary language of its traditional superstitions and irrationalities that we would be able to arrive at an entirely logical language that permitted only the positive—or truly objective—description of things. Such hopes were short-lived, however, for others—notably Nietzsche—had already asserted that the purpose of language was not simply to describe things as they are, but rather to assert how we would like them to be, even if they are not. Language, Nietzsche argued, is primarily an instrument of the will and not of the intellect *per se*, and as such language is not to be bound by the changing standards of logic or "objectivity," both of which are illusions deriving from a particular and historically conditioned philosophical world-picture; neither is language to be bound by standards of morality, which are invariably theologically grounded. Rather we must be left free to employ any and every device—indeed, even lies—as we project ourselves forward beyond the ebbing reifications of the past and the meaninglessness of all that simply *is*. "There is only *one* world," Nietzsche contends in *Will to Power*, "and this is false, cruel, contradictory, seductive, without meaning—a world thus constituted is the real world. *We have need of lies* in order to conquer this reality, this 'truth,' that is, in order to live—That lies are necessary in order to live is itself part of the terrifying and questionable character of existence."[43] In *Beyond Good and Evil*, Nietzsche contends that the proper task of the philosopher, therefore, is simply "to gain control of the many vain and fanciful interpretations and incidental meanings that have be scribbled and drawn over that eternal basic text of *homo natura* so far."[44] Describing Nietzsche's understanding of the philosophical task, Stephen Emmanuel writes:

> Nietzsche not only stresses the epistemological point that all knowing is limited by one's perspective, and hence that all interpretations are essentially incomplete; he goes on to claim that there are no rational grounds for believing in the existence of those things philosophers have traditionally employed to ground interpretations of self and world (including, preeminently, the concept of a Divine Author). Regarding the text of *homo natura* there can be no complete or final perspective, since all texts are constantly in the process of being rewritten. For Nietzsche, to "become master of the many vain and overly enthusiastic interpretations" means to have the courage to explore the limitless play of intertextuality, through which one acquires a deeper understanding of the textual labyrinth that is human existence.[45]

The incredulous posture that many postmodernist theorists now adopt with respect to words and speech thus suggests, on the one hand, that language is a prison from which we must try to escape by way of suspicion and "deconstruction," thereby ridding it of all traces of metaphysics and theology. Yet it also suggests that words and speech hold out the only hope of freedom, for language is instrumental in enabling us to express ourselves and our desires over and against the past as well as over and against the desires of others.

Viewed in a positive light, deconstructive theory simply aims to establish a kind of democracy of discourse in which no one voice is allowed to stifle any other and in which no one perspective on the truth is allowed to overshadow any other. Yet its critical and negating thrust would seem to be much more powerful. Indeed, much as Nietzsche's rant against the Christian religion—"the one immortal blemish upon the human race"[46]—appears to have left him willing to destroy everything for the sake of whatever the will-to-power might forcefully erect in the place of Christian civilization, so postmodernist hostility to metaphysics appears to leave contemporary theorists willing to risk everything for the sake of whatever might be constructed after a purely secular fashion. But this is both impatient and imprudent.[47] Indeed, the critics of modernity appear prepared to cast fate to the wind, assuming that anything must be better than the supposedly hierarchical and oppressive discourse of the Western tradition.

Yet what can possibly result from such imprudence except the triumph of strong interpretations over weak ones? In the context of increasingly powerful modern technologies, the strongest and most persuasive interpretations will very likely be those of technocrats, bureaucrats, and the managers of large corporations, in spite of Nietzsche's disdain for the "specialists without spirit" and "sensualists without heart." For notwithstanding the suggestion that we have entered a postmodern era, we continue to be surrounded by profoundly modern institutions that are animated by a number of successful and powerful modern interpretations of reality. Such interpretations have given rise—and will surely continue to give rise—to fateful scientific knowledge, to increasingly powerful techniques and technologies, and to increasingly effective trans-national corporate practices. Such typically modern developments must continue unchecked unless and until they are met with forcible moral and intellectual resistance. But what resistance will those who have become convinced that words and speech simply float on the surface of circumstance and desire be able to offer, say, to the continued development of genetic engineering techniques, or against the continued consolidation of trans-national corporations? One might just as well spit into a stiff headwind.

Finally, while it may be true that the appeal of radical postmodernist theory does not extend very far beyond graduate departments of English, an essentially deconstructive attitude is increasingly prevalent within contemporary culture, especially with respect to words and speech. This is evident in everything from news coverage to ordinary conversations. Bombarded by manipulative words we become tempted to hold language at arm's length. Yet our tolerance of monologue, as well as for those who contend that all speech is inevitably monological, may also betray our own complicity in the abuse of words and speech. Perhaps we wager that we stand to gain more from the abuse of language than we stand to lose. Perhaps language suffers today from much the same "tragedy of the commons" that has repeatedly led to the degradation of our environment, which is to say that each individual speaker of the common language doesn't consider his or her abuse of it to be of very much consequence and does not, in any event, want to find him or herself at a disadvantage by failing to keep up with all of the others who abuse it to their own advantage. It is for this reason that Roger Lundin characterizes contemporary American culture as a "culture of interpretation."

> What [it reveals] is a distinctly American pragmatism that is preoccupied with the usefulness of language, yet is skeptical about the power of language to reveal truth or to serve legitimately as an instrument of ethical obligation. Claiming that words point only to their origins in the individual or collective will, this contemporary pragmatism focuses upon language as an instrument of power and as a tool for the marketing of goods and services. In an "interpretive" culture as we now know it in the United States, the truthfulness of any idea is bound to appear secondary to its relevance, its marketability.[48]

Or perhaps we have become, just as Tocqueville feared, so narrowly focused on our own particular interests that we have lost a sense of how much monologue threatens our common life. Perhaps we believe that we can safely abandon public discourse to monologue even while protecting genuine dialogue in private. Yet even if this were possible, we do not as a culture appear to be any less pragmatic in our private use of words and speech than we are in our public use of them. On the contrary, it would seem that we are, if anything, even more permissive of manipulative speech in private.

Returning to Pieper's castigation of sophistry, it is instructive that he concludes his analysis by asserting that truth can only live in the words and speech of genuine conversation, and hence that well-ordered human existence—and particularly well-ordered social existence—depends upon well-ordered language.[49] Well-ordered language, he continues, requires staunch opposition to *anything* that threatens its capacity for disclosing the truth of things.

> [O]pposition is required, for instance, against every partisan simplification, every ideological agitation, every blind emotionality; against seduction through well-turned yet empty slogans, against autocratic terminology with no room for dialogue, against personal insult as an element of style (all the more despicable the more sophisticated it is), against the language of evasive appeasement and false assurance . . . and not least against categorical conformism, and categorical nonconformism.[50]

Of course, it is clear from the outset of Pieper's argument that he believes in the possibility of truthful speech because he believes that truth exists and that it is both intelligible and communicable. In spite of his discussion of Plato and the Sophists, furthermore, it is clear that Pieper believes these things because he is a Christian thinker and believes that God has spoken and continues to speak. While one obviously does not need to be a Christian to defend the possibility of truthful speech within contemporary culture, any attempt to mount opposition to monological speech today ought at least to be clear about the most radical source from which such opposition may be drawn, namely, the Christian theology of the *Word*. It is to this theology, then, that we turn in our final chapter.

4

A Theology of Dialogue

THE FOLLOWING PROPOSITION MIGHT be said to recapitulate our argument thus far: to the extent that words and speech have been corrupted within contemporary culture, there will be no escaping this corruption short of attempting to restore dialogue to health. Yet this proposition raises a number of awkward questions. Are we actually capable of dialogue? Do we have the courage to offer ourselves transparently to one another in genuine dialogue, owning up to and standing behind each of the words we speak to each other? Do we really even want to do this? I can only speak for myself at this point, but I often find it difficult to stand behind the words I speak, and I find that it is only the exceptional instance—and not, by any means, the rule—when I am able to offer myself transparently to someone else, even to those I love most deeply. I suspect that I am not alone in this difficulty.

The disconcerting noisiness of contemporary culture and the glut of impersonal information surrounding us surely accounts for some of the difficulty, as does the manipulative and depersonalizing effects of present-day sophistry, along with the postmodern suspicion that the flux of our experience and the tangle of our conflicting interests only very rarely—and at best accidentally—afford us the opportunity to really converse with one another. These cultural problems are serious impediments to genuine dialogue and go some distance toward explaining why we may have been tempted to lose our faith in words, why we so often back away from the words of others, and perhaps even why we fail to stand behind the words we speak.

Yet although the social and cultural analysis we have employed in our previous discussions is helpful, it cannot really account for the depth of our reluctance to open ourselves up to each other in genuine dialogue. Our reluctance is at once more immediate and more basic, stemming, I believe, from *fear*. We are at root deeply afraid of dialogue. In our weakness and confusion—indeed, in our sinfulness—we are afraid to reveal ourselves to each other. We have great difficulties facing up to this knowledge of ourselves. We find it easier and safer, in spite of all of the costs, to carry on living with appearances, with seeming, and with the opacity of ordinary conversation. We would even acquiesce to monological speech rather than risk the radical disclosure entailed in genuine dialogue. And we do all of these things by and large because we are afraid not to do them. If dialogue is ever to be restored to health, then, we will need somehow to overcome our fear.

But just what is it that are we afraid of? Is it simply that we will be despised or humiliated by others, or that we will expose ourselves to even more effective manipulation on the basis of our self-disclosure? Surely this must account for a good deal of our fear, for these are very real possibilities. Yet our reluctance to engage in dialogue runs still deeper than the fear and mistrust that we naturally and understandably have of each other. It extends to the real but rarely articulated fear that things *in general*—and not simply others—often seem indifferent and perhaps even inimical to our best interests and happiness. It stems from a generalized sense of insecurity in the world, a sense that we must guard ourselves, not simply from each other, but from the hazards and vicissitudes of life. We are, in short, deeply afraid of the impersonal, *anti*personal, and apparently inescapable forces that have for ages been lumped under the heading of *fate*. As Glenn Tinder observes in a provocative study entitled *Against Fate: An Essay on Personal Dignity*:

> Fate is all that threatens and befalls us. It comes upon us from without, often strange and uninvited, always at enmity with personal being. In words made commonplace by our familiarity with fate, it is "meaningless" or "absurd." Fate may be fragmented and appear in the form of disjointed circumstances, or it may be massive and unified, even predictable. It may be experienced in recurrent jolts or in situations that devour us. It is always alien and dangerous.[1]

Tinder goes on to observe that modern times have become peculiarly fateful, for embedded in the modern project is the fearful assumption that the nature of things is decidedly not ordered to our happiness and hence that things must be more-or-less violently made to serve our interests by means of such things as scientific and technological mastery. In effect, as Tinder suggests, modernity has sought to neutralize the threat of fate by means of human cleverness and the use of force. The various kinds of sophistry that we discussed in the last chapter might be said to reflect this modern thrust.

Still, while modern thinkers have regularly and repeatedly assured us that the rational-technical mastery of fate is both feasible and imminently realizable, we have begun to suspect that scientific and technological development may themselves be governed by fate, and that continued "progress" may pose an even more insidious threat to our lives than unmastered nature. Suspicions of this kind animate much of what today is discussed under the heading of postmodernism. And yet as correct as the hermeneutic of suspicion may be about many of the oppressive qualities of modern existence, it does next to nothing to allay our fear that life may in the end be meaningless and absurd. Indeed, it only exacerbates this fear, for radical postmodernist theory simply extends the typically modern assumption that meaning is something that we must willfully construct for ourselves to its logical—if depressing—conclusion. After critical theorists have finished deconstructing all of the supposedly oppressive metanarratives, and after they have eliminated the final remaining traces of metaphysics and theology from our habits of thought, they fall silent. Critical theory leaves us alone—or at best in small tribal groupings—to battle more-or-less hopelessly against the fates as best we can. Whatever strength we can muster for this battle, furthermore, must apparently stem from *ressentiment* and anxiety.

The contemporary situation is therefore one in which a great many of the older sources of hope seem to have been debunked, and in which a great many of us seem to find it increasingly difficult to believe that goodness is built into the order of things. Whereas traditional religious belief once affirmed that "Wisdom cries aloud from the streets, saying: 'Find me! Find life!'" we are tempted today to despair and to assume that there is, finally, nothing to hear. Certain theorists may find such radical incredulity liberating, even exhilarating, but it has left most of the rest of us increasingly cold and increasingly fearful. Most of us simply do not possess the mental and emotional fortitude to construe Nietzsche's text of *homo natura* and the ceaseless struggle for survival against the backdrop of chaos and meaninglessness as anything but very bad news. How can words and speech ever be anything *but* sophistry if this is really true?

The root problem confronting any attempt to recover meaningful dialogue, then, is not cultural or psychological or even ethical; rather it is metaphysical and ultimately *theological*. Can our world picture, and those basic assumptions we make about the way things *are*, make sense of Truth and Meaning? If not, there will be little point in going on about truthful or meaningful speech. Is existence finally amenable to us as personal agents? If not, then all attempts to defend personalizing speech must in the end come to naught. What— or, more crucially, *Who*—is responsible for our existence? Does God exist? Is God good? Can God be trusted? Unless all of these questions can be confidently answered in the affirmative, then there will be little point in stressing the importance of "I and Thou" relationality. Indeed, short of a theology that is able to account for the possibility of genuine dialogue, we have no hope of restoring dialogue to health. For want of such a theology, the best that we can hope for is simply the kind of liberal anarchy that permits each of us to do and to say whatever seems best and right in our own eyes. We appear to be moving rapidly toward just such a state of affairs at present with many contending that this is a good thing, better at least than the stifling homogeneity of modernist discourse. Perhaps it is, in certain respects. Yet anarchies are notoriously unstable and usually short-lived. A culture that tolerantly permits each one to do and to say whatever seems right in his or her own eyes is terribly vulnerable to the imposition of tyranny, a social fact well worth considering in light of powerful modern communications technologies. It must also be stressed that anarchy—even in an apparently benign liberal and tolerant form—is still largely inimical to genuine conversation, for no aggregation of monologues can ever produce a dialogue. Indeed, to the extent that we have dismissed the possibility of knowing and of speaking the *Truth*, we have already—though perhaps unwittingly—surrendered the possibility of coming to an understanding of *our* situation. We have made it all but impossible to say "*We.*"

Hence the successful recovery of dialogue can only be built upon a theological foundation that is able to bear the weight of such a recovery. As our previous discussions have shown, the postmodernist world picture, with its emphasis upon disorder and alterity, is not able to bear this weight, and neither is its modernist antecedent with its nearly exclusive stress upon abstract visualization. Basically, the preoccupation that both evince for taking control of things is not responsive to the posture of respectful listening that dialogue calls for. Their intrinsic secularity, furthermore, requires that they both ground truth and meaning finally in human willfulness. Monologue lies at the end of the trajectories of both modernism and postmodernism.

Many of those who have most constructively criticized the increasing objectification of contemporary life, therefore, and who have sought to redress the manipulative quality of contemporary thought, have done so in the name of a distinct alternative to both modern and postmodern worldviews and yet one with which Western thought is still vaguely familiar, namely, the predominantly *auditory* world picture of biblical theology.[2] There are, as we will see, a number of reasons for this, but one of the more important is that this theology does not place the noetic emphasis upon seeing as much as it does upon *listening*, and consequently upon speaking and acting on the basis of what has been *heard*. This is not to say that the authors of Scripture ignore the significance of visualization, for many of them speak on the basis of what they have seen, and the Scriptures are full of very profound pictures of the human situation. Yet relative to the classical philosophical and modern emphasis upon sight and seeing, the prophets and apostles are much more concerned that we should *listen*. Indeed, they assert that it will only be as we become sensitive to the voice of God that we will begin to see things as they really are. In his polemic directed against the *anti*-theology implicit in postmodern literary theory, for example, George Steiner contends: "[A]ny coherent account of the capacity of human speech to communicate meaning and feeling is, in the final analysis, underwritten by the assumption of God's presence."[3] It is underwritten, we must add, by the assumption that the God who is present is also One who *speaks*.

Logos versus dabhar

The difference between modern and biblical understanding is perhaps nowhere more clearly evident than in the different ways the two traditions conceive of the importance and purpose of words and ultimately in the different ways they understand the importance of the *Logos*, or the *Word*. Within the classical world picture, upon which the modernist worldview is largely based, the *Logos* concept pertains to the "order of things" and refers to the ultimate principle of being and animation. From the classical perspective, this primeval *Logos* is not a spoken word; neither is it heard so much as it is perceived within the mind's eye of rational reflection. To be sure, the *Logos* of classical philosophy is a dynamic concept, and yet it is wholly impersonal. Within the classical tradition, one does not expect to encounter the universe *personally*—as, say, when one encounters another or is addressed by another in dialogue—as much as one simply hopes to behold the eternal order of things, and if possible to comprehend it. The universe is thus pictured within the philosophical imagination as closed, at rest, and grounded ultimately in an eternal but impersonal principle of order. It is hardly surprising that the metaphors and models that the classical tradition has used to represent our knowledge of what *is* are largely visual and spatial.

While modern thinkers have tended to point the older classical view in a more activistic direction they have, as we have seen, remained largely committed to its predominantly visual noetic. Classical thinkers had hoped to be able to behold the order of things through rational reflection; modern thinkers have sought to disclose the underlying structure of things by way of active and often violent methods of inquiry. Modernity has thus placed the actively inquiring subject in the middle of a world of objects that passively wait to be illuminated, inspected, named, and used. The modern picture of the world, therefore, is not one in which we aspire to behold the light of the *Logos* shining through things as much as it is one in which we strive to *direct* the beam of enlightened intellect onto things in order to elucidate their inner workings for the sake of putting them to good use. In spite of this difference, however, modern understanding remains analogous to its classical antecedent in that it envisions the world as a finite text that is not to be heard so much as it is to be read or deciphered. It is a text furthermore that, while it can be re-arranged and engineered, cannot finally be altered, for it is ultimately governed by immutable physical laws. Hence although both the classical and the modern traditions place a great deal of stress upon trying to read the *Logos* inherent in things—witness our use of the terms bio*logy*, anthropo*logy*, psycho*logy*, etc.—neither tradition emphasizes the importance of the personal backing that words may or may not receive. Instead, the importance of words lies in their descriptive accuracy and/or heuristic usefulness.

The biblical tradition conceives matters differently. While the Bible also understands being primarily in terms of words, the principal stress is not placed upon reading these words for the sake of the kind of order they disclose, but rather upon hearing and speaking them for the sake of the covenants they establish. Persons and personal speech lie at the heart of biblical understanding. Along this line, the primary scriptural emphasis is placed upon hearing and obeying the words that *Yahweh* speaks, for he is the one who spoke and who continues to speak the creation into existence. "By the word *of the Lord* were the heavens made," the Psalmist proclaims, "their starry host by the breath of *his* mouth . . . For *he* spoke, and it came to be . . . *he* commanded, and it stood firm" (Ps 33:6, 9). Similarly, in the prologue to the fourth Gospel the apostle declares: "In the beginning was the Word, and the Word was with God, and the Word *was God*." While John employs the classical philosophical term *Logos*, he radically reinterprets and personalizes it after a characteristically Hebraic fashion. He wants his hearers to understand that the order of things has been brought forth by a God who *lives* and *acts* and *speaks*. Indeed, it is *Yahweh's* faithfulness to his own words that holds chaos at bay and not simply the fact that things have somehow been endowed with a principle of being and order. Furthermore, this living and speaking God has become flesh and dwelt among us as a human person, the Christ. The apostle Paul adopts a similar apologetic strategy in his address to the Athenians. Paul begins by appealing to vague religious sentiment but quickly moves on to proclaim a living God who creates, commands, calls, forgives, and who will ultimately judge the nations, by *"the breath of his mouth."* What the Athenians had hitherto worshipped in mute ignorance, Paul introduces as a God with whom it is possible to converse. Indeed, within the biblical tradition, speaking, declaring, commanding, conversing, promising, and warning are God's most characteristic actions. *Yahweh's* living, powerful presence in the world is thus not simply represented by the classical *Logos* concept, but also by the Hebrew word "*dabhar*," which has a variety of meanings all centered around the verb *to speak*. "[W]hoever has *dabhar*," Thorlief Boman writes in his seminal study, *Hebrew Thought Compared with Greek*, "knows Jahveh. *Dabhar* is more than a fragment, more than an emanation, or a hypostasis of the divinity; *dabhar* is a manifestation of Jahveh, and indeed the highest form of that manifestation. *Dabhar* is Jahveh as he is recognizable to mortal man (cf. Rom 1:20)."[4]

Within the biblical tradition, then, the principal object of understanding at present is not necessarily to see, nor is it somehow to behold the eternal order of things; rather it is to hear the voice of the One who has, by the breath of his mouth, spoken all things into being. Adam is thus said to have *heard* God calling to him in the cool of the day; Abram *heard* God's call to leave Haran and to go to the land the LORD would show him; Moses *heard* the voice from out of the burning bush; Elijah *heard* the gentle, whispering voice at the mouth of the cave; Jesus does nothing on his own but speaks only what the Father has *taught* him; and each of us is *called* to repentance and faith in Christ on the basis of having *heard* the gospel proclamation. Indeed, the only possible relationship that we can now have with God is premised upon *hearing his Word* and responding in faith and obedience. "Because you have seen me," Jesus told Thomas the doubter, "you have believed; but blessed are those who have not seen and yet have believed" (Jn 20:29). Nelly Villaneix has written beautifully along this line in an essay on Kierkegaard subtitled *La Voix et L'Ouïe* (The Voice and Hearing):

> [A]s early as Genesis God, for the creature, "is only a voice," that the eye cannot see, but that the ear can hear. To hear him is to be saved, since it is to receive the "efficacious," creative, and salvific Word. Also, all the prophets themselves mix the hardening of sin which makes one deaf to grace and the hardening of the ears. Revelation is nothing other than the "Word made flesh": the place where the eye fails to unveil the divine incognito. The ear can discern the "voice of the shepherd": "If anyone hears my voice . . ." From then on the role of man is clear: "Speak Lord, for your servant is listening." The ear is the channel through which revelation passes. It alone can, God willing, give the creature access to the "spiritual" universe. It is still hearing that allows him to remain in this spiritual universe by witnessing, it is said, by "confessing with his mouth" that which was first heard and, in turn, in this action, to hear. Thus, the faith comes from that which one hears: "How will they know unless someone speaks to them?" The disciple, the Christian, is therefore the one who places himself within the sound of the Word and who, for this reason, transmits it using his own word. It is the circulation of human words, humble gift to the other, which assumes the life of the "body of Christ": in their usage, in effect, the Word of God can resound and thus perpetuate the divine gift.[5]

Within the biblical tradition, furthermore, we do not discover the *Logos* by means of philosophical reflection or empirical investigation so much as we find ourselves *addressed by him*. This encounter is never simply an intellectual affair; it never arrives merely as information. Rather the divine address penetrates the heart in such a way as to elicit a deeply personal response, either one of faith and obedience or of turning away and covering the ears. "The word of God is living and active," the author of Hebrews writes along this line, "sharper than any double-edged sword, it penetrates even to dividing soul and spirit, joints and marrow; it judges the thoughts and attitudes of the heart" (Heb 4:12). The writer continues, "By faith we understand that the universe was formed at God's command, so that what is seen was not made out of what was visible.... And without faith it is impossible to please God, because anyone who comes to him must believe that he exists and that he rewards those who earnestly seek him" (Heb 11:3, 6).

Within the biblical tradition, therefore, we do not intuitively *see* the underlying principle of all things as much as we *believe* and *accept* words that are spoken into our hearts, words that reveal the One in whom we live and move and have our being. It is on the basis of these words alone that we are enabled to begin to see ourselves as we are and to see the world as it is. Hearing thus takes precedence over seeing, and it is through words and speech that the truth of things is disclosed. The words that matter most, furthermore, are not those of catalogued information and never those of manipulative monologue; rather, they are the words of dialogue, of God's address to us. These words never return to the One who utters them without having accomplished everything that he desires (Is 55:11), and yet they are the sorts of words that graciously permit the contingency of a genuinely personal response.

The Scriptures regularly and repeatedly contrast the living, speaking God with various and sundry "mute idols" that have mouths but cannot speak. *Yahweh's* powerful words, furthermore, are repeatedly contrasted with the empty words of those who make promises but cannot or will not fulfill them. Just as the Scriptures represent reality, true being, and concreteness in terms of *dabhar*, so they represent unreality, non-being, and emptiness with the word *lo-dabhar*, literally, "no-thing."[6] As Boman comments along this line, while "no-thingness" obviously has no positive being it can still exert an influence in our lives, an influence that is always negating, pernicious, and dangerous.[7] Indeed, although the lying words of the false prophets do not ultimately correspond to any positive reality, they are well able to deceive those who hear them and to divert those who receive them away from true being and into futility and "no-thingness." "A lie for the Hebrew," Boman writes:

> is not as it is for us, a non-agreement with the truth. . . .
> For him the lie is the internal decay and destruction of
> the word. . . . That which is powerless, empty, and vain
> is a lie: a spring which gives no water lies (Is 58:11,
> *kazabh*). For this reason, it is just as clear that the God
> of Israel does not lie (I Sam 15:29) as it is that the idols
> are lies (Jer 10:14). [8]

The biblical tradition also knows of words that, while they may not be lies *per se*, nevertheless lack the inner strength of realization.[9] Such are the words of false prophets which, though perhaps well-intended and reassuring, are presumptuous, empty, and contribute to *lo-dabhar*, to "no-thingness."

To be sure, the prophets and apostles repeatedly enjoin us to seek out the order of things and to marvel at how well the world has been ordered. Yet this is not so that we will stand in awe of the created order *per se*, but rather that we would return words of praise and thanksgiving to the One who has so wisely and graciously ordered them. "Let everything that has breath," the psalmist charges in Psalm 150, "praise the LORD. Praise the LORD!" While nature may well be described as a kind of finite text within this tradition, and while this text can after a fashion be read, the meaning and purpose of this text is ultimately to reflect the glory of its *Author*. The words that we speak become meaningful, furthermore, not simply by reproducing aspects of an impersonal and immutable text, but rather as, William Poteat suggests, by being "expressions of the personal, to *our* ears entirely mutable, but, in secret, unfailingly self-consistent intentions of Yahweh, the speaker and actor par excellence."[10]

This biblical theology of *dabhar* has any number of critical implications for our understanding of the purpose of words and speech, and it underscores the importance of assuming a dialogical posture with respect to them. In the first instance, it suggests that speaking and listening—core elements of our actual experience as persons—are not simply biological or socio-cultural accidents. On the contrary, this theology suggests that our capacity for speaking and listening—for dialogue—is precisely what links us most closely to God, to the one who has spoken all things into being. Indeed, speaking and listening have as solid an ontological basis as it is possible to imagine. That we are able to enter into conversation with each other, furthermore, is evidence of our dignity as having been created after God's likeness and image. We will return to this point in a moment, but suffice it here simply to say that our capacity for dialogue is, according to the biblical theology of *dabhar*, perhaps God's greatest gift to humanity.

The biblical theology of *dabhar* also suggests that words and speech do not merely disclose the order of things, but that they actually establish it. This theology suggests that being rests upon the covenant that the one who spoke and continues to speak the world into existence has made to stand behind his words.

The tradition further maintains that the stability and coherence of the *worlds* that we construct with our own words depends in large part upon the faithfulness with which we speak them. That our verbally created *worlds* have not collapsed into "no-thingness" in spite of our carelessness and deceitfulness should not tempt us to believe that our words are of relatively little value. Rather the continuing existence of our *worlds* in spite of our carelessness is yet another indication of God's ongoing commitment to his own words of creation, as well as of his long-suffering patience with us. In his grace, God does not allow our situations to dissolve completely into the "no-thingness" toward which our empty words tend. But we should not presume upon such grace, for the place—if it can even be called that—of *lo-dabhar* will be hell.

The auditory world picture entailed in the biblical theology of *dabhar* is also very clearly one in which there is room for contingency, for within this world picture what *is* and what *will be* are entirely contingent upon what is said and done.[11] Of course, what *is* and what *will be* are most obviously contingent upon what *Yahweh* says and therefore does, but what *is* and what *will be* are also mysteriously contingent upon what we say in response to him as well as to others. The created order of things, in other words, has not been so tightly scripted that we cannot speak freely and, as it were, *impromptu*. As William Poteat suggests,

> If reality is conceived after the analogy of the speaking *dabhar* of Yahweh, the paradigmatic speaker, then it follows that the world's existence as such, as well as each and every one of its particulars, is *absolutely* contingent, even as God's faithful ownership of his actual and particular words and deeds is *absolutely* contingent—that is, *absolutely* equally liable to happen

or not happen. At the same time, however, though these words and deeds of God are radically underivable from any eternally binding *regulae*; and though the way in which these are implicated with his identity as "I will be that I will be" is not a priori searchable; *this absolute* contingency is not the contingency of the absolutely random—which . . . could not be recognized even, were it, *per impossible*, to exist—but rather is that of the *unconditioned personal act addressed to other persons: personally owned words before an other* who takes them up and covenants himself with them.[12]

Indeed, because *Yahweh* has identified himself as "I will be that I will be," he reveals himself to be faithfulness,[13] completely obviating our age-old fear of fate. We need now only fear—in the sense of taking care—to attend to the One whose voice, as the psalmist declares, "breaks in pieces the cedars of Lebanon" and "strikes with flashes of lightning" (Ps 29:5, 7).

The introduction into the ancient world of the conviction that reality is personally and subjectively established was an ontological development of enormous historical importance.[14] The classical world picture in which reality was held to be impersonally established contained relatively little space for the power of dialogical speech to be realized. It was the biblical world picture that, as many have noted, first allowed spirit and self-consciousness to appear fully in history.[15] The goodness and utter reliability of the *Word* so emphasized within the biblical tradition also had the effect, as mentioned above, of controverting the fatefulness of ancient thought. For although the God proclaimed in the Scriptures is awesome and at times terrifying, he is neither capricious nor arbitrary. Not only are the forces and agencies of chaos firmly under his control, but he makes them to serve his good purposes.

Returning to our initial observation that fear is perhaps the most serious obstacle confronting the recovery of dialogue, the world proclaimed in the biblical theology of *dabhar* is one in which faithfulness and trustworthiness—core aspects of genuine dialogue—are underwritten by a God who cannot lie and whose purposes cannot be thwarted even by those who do lie. Such a conviction completely undermines the fearful temptation to believe that we cannot risk speaking truthfully or, alternatively, the despairing temptation to assume that "meaning" lies only in the eye of the beholder.

To say that the *imago dei* and the human faculties of listening and speaking find a basis in the theology of *dabhar* is not yet to tell the whole story, however, for dialogue and dialogical existence have their foundation, finally, in God's triune and intra-communicative nature. It is the revelation that *Yahweh* is and has always been one God in three Persons—Father, Son, and Spirit—that ultimately grounds the possibility of dialogue. This is of critical importance. For the *Word* could not be said to be a genuinely dialogical word, in the sense that we have developed, if in the final analysis God is alone as a speaker. Real communicative freedom and contingency—core elements of dialogue—could not be real human possibilities had they not already existed in the conversation that has eternally united the Father, the Son, and the Spirit. Admittedly, the nature of this conversation is a deep mystery. Yet to back away from it in the direction of monism or unitarianism can only lead to the supposition that God must somehow need the world in order to have something to speak to and that he has only been able to become himself on the basis of the emanation of a dialogical partner. This view—such as we find, for example, in the influential philosophy of Hegel—implies that freedom and contingency are finally illusory and that what appears to be a genuine dialogue between God and humankind is really only an expression of something like what Hegel termed "the cunning of reason."[16] Traditional orthodoxy has affirmed to the contrary that God does not need the world, but rather that he has created the world out of an abundance of the love shared eternally by the Father, the Son, and the Holy Spirit. Christian theology has understood the apostolic assertion that "God is love" (1 Jn 4:8, 16) to be an ontological assertion and not simply to modify God's character, as if simply to say that God is "loving." Love is not something that God creates; it is the essence of his existence. Love describes the basic quality of the relations that have eternally united the Father, the Son, and the Holy Spirit.

And the same must also be said of dialogue. Indeed, just as God is love, so we may also say that God is *conversation*. The possibility of dialogue is not simply something that God has created. Rather dialogue describes his essentially intra-communicative nature. As Luther observed: "God, too, in his majesty and nature, is pregnant with a Word or a conversation in which He engages with Himself in His divine essence and which reflects the thoughts of His heart. This is as complete and excellent and perfect as God Himself."[17] Or, as T. F. Torrance has written more recently: "In his own eternal Essence God is not mute or dumb, but Word communicating or speaking himself. That is the Word which we hear in the Holy Scriptures, which works or effects in us through the Spirit intuitive, auditive, evident knowledge of God."[18] God's triune self-communication, in short, is the ground and grammar for all true communication.[19]

Returning to our earlier point linking the possibility of dialogue with the *imago dei*, we can say that what makes us truly human is precisely that we have been invited by God to enter into the kind of genuinely personal dialogue—the "I and Thou" encounter realized only in speaking and listening—that has been eternally shared by the Father with the Son and with the Holy Spirit.[20] As Ronald Hall writes:

> [H]erein may be the heart of the human *imago dei*: the human likeness to God is found in the human capacity to hear God's address and to answer it, in the capacity to own and to own up to one's words—a capacity that enables humans to sustain and to stabilize what they have brought forth, a capacity that enables them to transform the dynamic flux of temporality into the order of historical continuity.[21]

In speaking of our capacity to "sustain and stabilize" what we have brought forth, Hall's comments underscore the importance of naming, the full significance of which we are now in a position to appreciate in light of the biblical theology of *dabhar.* To name is to do more than to simply recognize and to verbalize what *is*; it is to enter into relation with what is named and thus to bring something fundamentally new into being. Our naming is not to create *ex nihilo*, of course, for our words are always spoken within a creation that has already been brought forth and is faithfully sustained in existence by God's creative *Word.* Yet our naming is genuinely creative and genuinely free. Ronald Hall describes this derivative yet genuinely creative capacity in terms of "qualified nominalism," which he contrasts to traditional realism. He writes:

> If we were to assume a *dabhar* interpretation of language then a qualified nominalism becomes plausible. Here there are no realities independent of their names, no sense in which realities exist in any determinate way prior to the naming process. At the same time, on

this interpretation, names refer to realities in a much closer ontological sense than in realism, for here the naming context is essential in the process of bringing the real forth into its determinate actuality. And so, on this *dabhar* interpretation . . . the long and the short of the answer to the question "What is in a name?" is an unequivocal "Everything!"[22]

As those created after the image and likeness of God, in other words, it has been given to us to usher the created order even more fully into being by naming it as well as to participate in sustaining what we have named by way of covenantal "response-ability." This is the essence of our stewardship over creation. While we derive the strength and capacity to do this from *Yahweh's* original *dabhar*, the *world* of meaning that we construct is still truly ours. For our *world* to truly sustain life, however, it must remain consonant with the wisdom—the *Logos*—embedded within created order. To the extent that we find ourselves able to speak meaningfully and truthfully, therefore, this is because it has been given to us to exercise dominion over a created order that is already pregnant with life and meaning. As Steiner writes:

> Does this mean that all adult *poiesis*, that everything we recognize as being of compelling stature in literature, art, music is of a religious inspiration or reference? As a matter of history, of pragmatic inventory, the answer is almost unequivocal. Referral and self-referral to a transcendent dimension, to that which is felt to reside either explicitly—that is to say ritually, theologically, by force of revelation—or implicitly, outside immanent and purely secular reach, does underwrite created forms from Homer and the *Oresteia* to *The Brothers*

Karamozov and Kafka. It informs art from the caves at
Lascaux to Rembrandt and to Kandinsky.[23]

The biblical theology of *dabhar*—of the God who has spoken
and continues to speak—thus entails a world picture (which is
obviously no longer the right description) within which words
are of paramount importance. It is a world picture in which
God's greatest joy is to speak to us and to enter into dialogue
with us.[24] It is also one in which the principal test of ourselves
as human persons is the extent to which we own our words,
stand behind them, and are present in them before each other.[25]
As we said at the outset, words are the very stuff of our lives; to
back away from them is to back away from life itself.

This biblical world picture is also one in which the primary
human task in the world is not to speak, but rather to listen.
It is to listen for the voice of the living God and to respond
faithfully and obediently to his address. In short, it suggests
that we must learn, as Luther once put it, "to see with our
ears." Along this line, it would be difficult to exaggerate the
importance that the authors of Scripture attach to listening.
Again and again the prophets and apostles implore us to listen
to the voice of God. The refrain *"Shema!"* "Listen!" runs right
through both Testaments, from Moses's recitation of *Torah*,
"Hear, O Israel, and be careful to obey so that it may go
well with you" (Deut 6:3); to the Psalmist's declaration, "The
entrance of your words gives light" (Ps 119:20); to the urgently
repeated prophetic entreaty, "Listen, listen to me, and eat what
is good.... Give ear and come to me; hear me, that your soul
may live" (Is 55:2); to Jesus's assertion, "It is written: Man does
not live by bread alone, but on every word that comes from the
mouth of God" (Mt 4:4); to the apostolic exhortation, "Today,
if you hear his voice, do not harden your hearts" (Heb 3:7); and
to the apocalyptic overture of the risen Christ, "If anyone hears

my voice and opens the door, I will go in and eat with him and he with me" (Rev 3:20).

Of course, there was a time when the *Word* became flesh and dwelt among us and was clearly visible to all those who had eyes to see, and there will also come a time when we will all see him face to face. For the present, however, our knowledge of God, and hence of who we are before him, is attained primarily by hearing and only very rarely by seeing. In striking contrast to the visual bias of contemporary culture, then, biblical theology announces that the truth of things is, for the present, something that can only be heard.[26] As Nelly Viallaneix has written:

> [H]earing is thus the privileged organ of sense which, making possible the relation of God to man, allows at the same time, the fraternal relations of men one with another. To forget this leads to a degeneration of language, that is to say, a cultural and religious crisis. To remember this hastens the coming of the "new heaven" and of the "new earth," where there will no longer be "weeping and gnashing of teeth," but deep harmony.[27]

Sadly, it seems that we have in fact forgotten this, and that our forgetfulness has indeed led to the degeneration of language and to cultural and religious crises of all kinds. We have become, as Kierkegaard put it so frankly in Danish, "*dumme,*" that is, deaf and stupid with respect to hearing God's voice. The racket of empty, impersonal, and depersonalizing speech has only made this problem worse. It has become all but impossible for us to hear the voice of God.

Yet we would be mistaken to simply attribute our deafness to the noisiness of contemporary culture, as if the problem were somehow new and soluble simply by way of escape. Rather the problem of human deafness may be said to be archetypical, with roots extending all the way back to the original fall from grace. Reflecting on the Genesis account of Adam and Eve's original disobedience, Kierkegaard contended that sin is ultimately what accounts for our stubborn preference for the visible and for our continuing negligence with respect to listening. Viallaneix recounts Kierkegaard's argument as follows:

> Evoking the lost Paradise, [Kierkegaard] depicts the relation established by the Creator with humanity, his creatures, as a harmonious relation. The Word of God holds it. With all his being, man listens. It is said that he obeys, since to hear and to obey: *akouo*, is all one.... [Yet] the Fall arrived unexpectedly. A sudden deafness prevented man from hearing the word addressed to him: "Has God really spoken to him? . . ." Then doubt suddenly appeared. No longer recognizing the Word, man no longer recognized himself. He no longer knew himself. He entered a universe that seemed absurd to him. This perturbation of the primary auditory relation of obedience bent itself into a relation of opposition, the relation of love transformed itself, deformed itself, into a ego twisting in on itself.[28]

While we have not lost the capacity to love, we have diverted love from its original object and we love ourselves inordinately. While we have not lost our capacity to know, or to use our reason, or to hear, we have separated all of these from love. We have diverted these capacities and assigned failure or limitation to them. The original auditory relation that Kierkegaard described has thus devolved into an abstract conceptual relation. Our reason no longer frees us from the appearances and illusions formed by the visual bias of speculative thought, but simply describes these appearances in ever greater detail, reinforcing our dependence upon and captivity to them. In effect, our eyes have overcome our ears, entirely reversing the original relation of hearing and seeing.[29] This reversal has left us captive to seeming, to appearances, and to the spirit of comparison, rivalry, and envy that dominate the present age. The human condition may thus be described in terms of hypocrisy and idolatry—hypocrisy severing what is said from the inner life of the one who speaks, and idolatry constraining our ability to trust only in that which is visible and manipulable.

Perhaps the most egregious manifestation of this triumph of the eye over the ear is the willful determination to use the power of speech—the essential medium of spiritual existence—to subvert the possibility of hearing the voice of God, to use words and language to evade and to actively negate the possibility of "response-ability" before God. Such a denial, Hall writes, is demonic:

> [The] demonic individual avoids worldly bonds by turning the very resource for establishing these bonds, namely words themselves, into empty talk. Such empty talk, such prattle, conceals rather than reveals, dis-integrates rather than integrates; in this empty talk—this incessant talk—an ironic and deeper silence is revealed. Here there is a retreat from the world by means of a subtle retreat from words, a retreat accomplished by a constant detachment and absence of the "speaker" from the words he utters. Here the demonic individual gushes forth with words, he waxes eloquent in poetry and lyricism, and his rhapsody is as seductive as music; indeed this is because his words have become music! But in all of this sound and fury, nothing is said; here the "speaker" flees from himself, from freedom, from integrity, from presence, from continuity, from every worldly bond, by flirting with

the very means through which these find their concrete actualization, namely, speech itself.[30]

The fact that our culture has become full of empty—in effect, "musical"—speech indicates a desperate indifference to responsible personal existence. Indeed, in spite of its apparent fullness, the noisiness of contemporary culture discloses a profound emptiness, a kind of "sonic desert"[31] within which genuinely personalizing speech may from time to time be voiced but can hardly be heard because it is so quickly drowned out by the ubiquitous din. Our situation recalls the prophecy of Amos: "'The days are coming,' declares the Sovereign LORD, 'when I will send a famine through the land—not a famine of food or a thirst for water, but a famine of hearing the words of the LORD'" (Amos 8:11). The sense of the text is not that the words are not there to be heard, but rather that we will have become incapable of hearing them because it has simply become too noisy. With precisely this problem in mind, Kierkegaard wrote,

> If I were a physician and someone asked me "What do you think should be done?" I would answer, "The first thing, the unconditional condition for anything to be done, consequently the very first thing that must be done is: create silence, bring about silence; God's word cannot be heard, and if in order to be heard in the hullabaloo it must be shouted deafeningly with noisy instruments, then it is not God's Word; create silence! Ah, everything is so noisy; and just as strong drink is said to stir the blood, so everything in our day, even the most insignificant project, even the most empty communication, is designed merely to jolt the senses or to stir up the masses, the crowd, the public, noise! And man, this clever fellow, seems to have become sleepless in order to invent ever new instruments to

increase noise, to spread noise and insignificance with the greatest possible haste and on the greatest possible scale. Yes, everything is soon turned upside down: communication is indeed soon brought to its lowest point with regard to meaning, and simultaneously the means of communication are indeed brought to their highest with regard to speedy and overall circulation; for what is publicized with such hot haste and, on the other hand, what has greater circulation than— rubbish! Oh, create silence!"[32]

The first thing we must do, then, is to somehow place ourselves in the position of being able to hear God's voice, of being able to listen. This is where the recovery of dialogue must begin. It will only be as we learn to listen to the voice of God—in the Scriptures, in the church, in creation, in our own hearts—that we will begin to regain confidence in the power of words and speech to establish a world within which it will be possible for us and for others to live. When we do venture to speak, furthermore, we must strive to do so soberly, faithfully, and covenantally. For if we are not careful to utter responsible and truthful words, we will inevitably utter empty and harmful ones, thereby contributing to the *lo-dabhar* or "no-thingness" that cannot sustain life and will ultimately be condemned by the *Word* upon his return. Speaking is a great joy, but it is also a serious business. It is to take a stand in the world, to actualize ourselves as human persons before God and before each other. While empty speech tears down and foolish words ensnare the soul and endanger others, good words echo, as we have seen, the original *dabhar* by bringing forth and sustaining a world in which it is possible for persons to live and flourish. "LORD, who may dwell in your sanctuary?" David queries in Psalm 15. He goes on to declare: "He whose walk is blameless and who does what is righteous, who speaks the truth from his heart and has no slander on his tongue, who does his neighbor no wrong and casts no slur on his fellow man, who despises a vile man but honors those who fear the LORD, who keeps his oath even when it hurts, who lends his money without usury and does not accept a bribe against the innocent. He who does these things will never be shaken." We must pray, then, as David goes on to pray in Psalm 19, that God in his mercy will forgive our hidden faults, that he will not allow our sins to rule over us, and that he will graciously find the words of our mouths and the meditation of our hearts pleasing in his sight.

Epilogue

IN THE FIRST CHAPTER of his Gospel, Luke writes that the angel Gabriel appears to Zechariah in the temple as the elderly priest offers incense on the altar. The angel announces to Zechariah that Elizabeth, his aged and barren wife, will soon conceive and will bear him a son. Zechariah is understandably frightened. He is also skeptical. "How can I be sure of this?" he asks. "I am an old man and my wife is well along in years." On account of his incredulity, Zechariah is rendered mute until the prophecy is fulfilled some months later. He regains the power of speech only after he names the child "John" as the angel had commanded him.

Luke also writes that God sent the angel Gabriel to Nazareth to announce to Mary that she was to become the mother of Jesus, the Christ. "How can this be," Mary asks the angel, "since I am a virgin?" Mary is told that the child she will bear will be conceived by the power of the Holy Spirit, that her cousin Elizabeth is also going to have a child in her old age, and that nothing is impossible with God. Mary consents to Gabriel's announcement and gives herself to the actualization of his prophecy with the words: "I am the LORD's servant. May it be to me as you have said." Some time later, Elizabeth honors Mary's courage and humility by declaring: "Blessed is she who has believed that what the LORD has said to her will be accomplished!" Thereafter follows Mary's song, the *Magnificat*, one of the most beautiful hymns of praise in the Bible.

In addition to writing an orderly account of these events, it would seem that Luke intends to contrast these overlapping stories, particularly Zechariah's and Mary's differing responses to the words delivered to them by the angel Gabriel. In certain respects their responses are quite similar. Both Zechariah and Mary are startled by the appearance of the angel, and both are frightened. Both ask questions. Yet Zechariah is chastised for not believing Gabriel's words and he is punished with muteness for a period of months. By contrast, Mary is commended for believing the angel and for humbly giving herself to the LORD's service. Her trusting consent issues forth in uncommonly beautiful speech.

The two stories also convey the sovereignty of the divine address. Gabriel does not suggest that the events will take place *if* Zechariah and Mary consent to the messages he bears. Both messages are delivered in the indicative. The events will unfold just as the words of the angel's prophecy, words he has been sent to speak, reveal. Yet the manner in which the prophecies are delivered is clearly not meant to overwhelm the two recipients. Both are clearly known to God. In Zechariah's case the address is said to have come in answer to his prayer; Mary is greeted with that assurance that she has found favor with God. Both are told not to fear; both are allowed to ask questions; both receive answers appropriate to the questions they have asked. Both interactions, though brief, are thus genuinely dialogical in the sense that we have developed. Yet the text indicates that Mary's response of trust and consent—"I am the LORD's servant. May it be to me as you have said"—is particularly felicitous. Her response gives rise to great joy and to beautiful words, words that continue to be sung around the world week by week in the Church's liturgy. Zechariah also eventually sings a song, and it is also quite beautiful. Yet the text indicates that his tongue was only loosed to sing after a long period of agonizing silence, in which he was unable to tell anyone what had he had been told or that God was soon to fulfill the promises he had made to Abraham. Zechariah's initial failure to believe the angel's words, apparently due to his reluctance to believe that God was capable of enabling an elderly woman to bear a child, had rendered him unable to speak.

This intriguing contrast of two possible responses to the divine address provides us, I believe, with an important clue as to how we might begin to pull genuine dialogue out from beneath the burden of catalogue and monologue. This recovery can only begin as we place ourselves in a position of being able to hear God's voice, of believing the words that he speaks to us, and of believing, as the angel assured Mary, that truly nothing is impossible with God. Our recovery of dialogue must begin, in short, in *faith*.

Surely, this should not surprise us. The recovery of dialogue does not, in the first instance, depend upon our cleverness; neither does it depend upon our strength of character. Dialogue has never, finally, depended upon us. Indeed, if our words have ever enabled us to build up a common *world*, to say *we*, or to experience the happiness that is perfected by gratitude; if our words have been able to bear *any* fruit at all in this world, this has always been because we have been allowed—by God's grace—to participate in the creative potency of the divine *Word*. If we are to recover genuine dialogue from beneath the suffocating weight of catalogue and monologue, we must listen to the One by whose breath the heavens and earth were made and by whose *Word* our world continues to be held in existence.

We must rediscover, in short, what it means to see with our ears.

When we venture to speak, we need only strive to turn to each other in truth, standing behind and owning up to the words we utter. Dialogue requires no more than this and no less. Will this be easy? No. Will it be worth the effort? Absolutely! For our efforts will surely—by the grace of God—be rewarded with the "*We*" of genuine fellowship, both in this age and in the age to come.

Notes

Prologue

[1] George Steiner, *Real Presences* (Chicago: University of Chicago Press, 1989), 58.

[2] Robert Mitchell, *Less Than Words Can Say* (Boston: Little, Brown & Co., 1979). Mitchell writes: "Two things . . . are necessary for intelligent discourse: an array of names and a conventional system for telling. The power of a language is related, therefore, to the size and subtlety of its lexicon, its bank of names, and the flexibility and accuracy of its telling system, its grammar" (192).

[3] See Martin Buber, *The Knowledge of Man: A Philosophy of the Interhuman* (New York: Harper & Row, 1965), chapter 2: "Distance and Relation," 59ff.

[4] This is one of Robert Mitchell's central contentions in *Less Than Words Can Say.*

[5] Buber, *The Knowledge of Man*, 108.

[6] St. Augustine, *The Greatness of the Soul & The Teacher* (New York: Newman Press, 1978), 147.

Chapter 1

[1] Martin Heidegger, "The Origin of the Work of Art" (1935), translated by Albert Hofstadter, in *Martin Heidegger: Basic Writings*, edited by David Farrell Krell (New York: HarperSanFrancisco, 1993), 198.

[2] See, for example, Edward Sapir, "Language," in *Culture, Language and Personality: Selected Essays*, edited by David G. Mandelbaum (Berkeley: University of California Press, 1962), 1–44.

[3] Walker Percy, *The Message in the Bottle: How Queer Man Is, How Queer Language Is, and What One Has to Do with the Other* (New York: Farrar, Straus & Giroux, 1954), 203. Percy cites the work of Sapir.

[4] Ibid.

[5] Ibid.

[6] Emile Benveniste, "Subjectivity in Language," translated by Mary Elizabeth Meek, in *Philosophy of Language: The Big Questions*, edited by Andrea Nye (Oxford: Blackwell, 1998), 47.

[7] George Steiner, *Real Presences* (Chicago: University of Chicago Press, 1989), 56.

[8] Benveniste, "Subjectivity in Language," 48.

[9] Ibid.

[10] George Steiner, *After Babel: Aspects of Language and Translation*, 3rd ed. (Oxford: Oxford University Press, 1998), 101–102.

[11] Benveniste, "Subjectivity in Language," 49.

[12] Ibid., 47.

[13] Blaise Pascal, *Pensées*, translated by A. J. Krailsheimer (New York: Penguin, 1966), 56–57.

[14] Percy, *The Message in the Bottle*, 257.

[15] Benveniste, "Subjectivity in Language," 48.

[16] Martin Buber, *The Eclipse of God: Studies in the Relation Between Religion and Philosophy* (New York: Harper & Row, 1952), 40.

[17] Martin Buber, *The Knowledge of Man: A Philosophy of the Interhuman*, translated by Maurice Friedman and Ronald Gregor Smith (New York: Harper & Row, 1965), 106.

[18] William H. Poteat, *Polanyian Meditations: In Search of a Post-Critical Logic* (Durham, NC: Duke University Press, 1985), 168.

[19] Steiner, *Real Presences*, 53.

[20] Hans Georg Gadamer, *Truth and Method*, trans. Joel Weinsheimer and Donald G. Marshall, 2nd ed. (New York: Continuum, 1997), 414.

[21] Ibid., 385.

[22] Poteat, *Polanyian Meditations*, 95.

[23] Ibid.

[24] Buber, *The Knowledge of Man*, 86.

[25] Ibid., 79.

[26] Ibid., 69. Note: Buber's original wording has been modified in the interest of gender inclusiveness.

[27] Ibid., 77.

[28] Ibid.

[29] Ibid., 78–79.

[30] Ibid., 108.

[31] Ibid.

[32] Søren Kierkegaard, *Concluding Unscientific Postscript*, translated by David F. Swenson and Walter Lowrie (Princeton: Princeton University Press, 1941 [1846]), 317.

[33] This is George Steiner's central thesis in *Real Presences*.

[34] Nietzsche cited in Alasdair MacIntyre, *Three Rival Versions of Moral Inquiry: Encyclopedia, Genealogy, and Tradition* (Notre Dame, IN: University of Notre Dame Press, 1990), 35.

[35] See, for example, Nicholas Wolterstorff's discussion of Jacques Derrida in *Divine Discourse: Philosophical Reflections on the Claim that God Speaks* (Cambridge: Cambridge University Press, 1995). "Derrida," Wolterstorff writes, "is metaphysics' relentless, indefatigable, fight-to-the-death opponent; his brief against discourse interpretation is that it is metaphysical . . . . So what does Derrida have in mind by 'metaphysics'? The core of metaphysics, as he understands it, is the assumption of *presence*. Metaphysics represents the determination of Being as *presence* in all sense of this word. It could be shown that all names related to fundamentals, to principles, or to the center have always designated an invariable presence—*eidos, arche, telos, energia, ousia* (essence, existence, substance, subject) *aletheia*, transcendentality, consciousness, God, man, and so forth . . . . *Meaning*, claims Derrida, *is a creature of signification*. It does not exist anterior to signification" (156–157).

[36] See Kenneth R. Miller, *Finding Darwin's God: A Scientist's Search for Common Ground Between God and Evolution* (New York: Harper Collins, 1999), 176ff.

[37] Stephen Jay Gould cited in Miller, *Finding Darwin's God*, 177.

[38] Buber, *The Knowledge of Man*, 117

[39] Nelly Viallaneix, "Søren Kierkegaard: La Voix et L'Ouïe (A Propos des Quatre Discours Edifiants de 1843)," in *Les Etudes Philosophiques* (Janvier-Mars, 1969): 211-224, unpublished translation by Paul Martens (1999).

⁴⁰ *The Westminster Confession of Faith & The Larger and Shorter Catechisms* (Inverness, U.K.: Free Presbyterian Press, 1981), 129.

Chapter 2

¹ Walker Percy, *The Message in the Bottle: How Queer Man Is, How Queer Language Is, and What One Has to Do with the Other* (New York: Farrar, Straus & Giroux, 1954), 119–149.

² Ibid., 119.

³ Ibid., 144.

⁴ Søren Kierkegaard, *Concluding Unscientific Postscript* (Princeton, NJ: Princeton University Press, 1941 [1846]), 20.

⁵ Alexander Nehamas, "Lofty Ideas That May Be Losing Altitude," in *The New York Times*, November 1, 1997.

⁶ See, for example, Friedrich Nietzche, *The Anti-Christ*, translated by H. L. Mencken (Tuscon, AZ: See Sharp Press, 1999). Nietzsche writes, "When the center of gravity of life is placed *not* in life itself, but in 'the beyond'—in *nothingness*—then one has taken away its center of gravity altogether. The vast lie of personal immortality destroys all reason, all natural instinct— henceforth, everything in the instincts that is beneficial, that fosters life, and that safeguards the future is a cause of suspicion. So to live that life no longer has any meaning: *this* is now the 'meaning' of life" (61).

⁷ Kierkegaard, *Concluding Unscientific Postscript*, 223.

⁸ *The Compact Oxford English Dictionary*, 2nd ed. (Oxford: Clarendon Press, 1989), 221.

⁹ C. S. Lewis, *Studies in Words*, 2nd ed. (Cambridge: Cambridge University Press, 1960), 313.

¹⁰ Marshall McLuhan, *The Gutenberg Galaxy: The Making of Typographic Man* (New York: Signet, 1969), 195.

¹¹ Jacques Ellul, *The Humiliation of the Word*, translated by Joyce Main Hanks (Grand Rapids, MI: Eerdmans, 1985), 11.

¹² Martin Buber, *The Eclipse of God: Studies in the Relation Between Religion and Philosophy* (New York: Harper & Row, 1952), 31.

¹³ Ronald L. Hall, *Word and Spirit: A Kierkegaardian Critique of the Modern Age* (Bloomington, IN: Indiana University Press, 1993), 21.

¹⁴ Hans Georg Gadamer, *Truth and Method* (New York: Continuum, 1997 [1960]), 413–414.

[15] Thorlief Boman, *Hebrew Thought Compared With Greek*, translated by Jules L. Moreau (New York: W. W. Norton, 1960), 67.

[16] Susan. A. Handelman, *The Slayers of Moses: The Emergence of Rabbinic Interpretation in Modern Literary Theory* (Albany, NY: S.U.N.Y. Press, 1982), 5.

[17] Boman, *Hebrew Thought Compared With Greek*, 67.

[18] McLuhan, *Gutenberg Galaxy*, 38.

[19] Descartes cited in John Passmore, *Man's Responsibility for Nature: Ecological Problems and Western Traditions* (London: Gerald Duckworth and Co., 1974), 20.

[20] Thomas. F. Torrance, *Theology in Reconstruction* (Eugene, OR: Wipf & Stock, 1996), 66.

[21] Ibid.

[22] Walter J. Ong, *Interfaces of the Word: Studies in the Evolution of Consciousness and Culture* (Ithaca, NY: Cornell University Press, 1977), 124–125.

[23] Ibid., 140.

[24] Ibid., 135.

[25] George Steiner, *Language and Silence: Essays on Language, Literature, and the Inhuman* (New Haven: Yale University Press, 1998 [1958]), 15.

[26] George Steiner, *Real Presences* (Chicago: University of Chicago, 1989), 114.

[27] Thomas F. Torrance, *Reality and Scientific Theology* (Edinburgh: Scottish Academic Press, 1985), 195.

[28] Steiner, *Real Presences*, 115.

[29] William H. Poteat, *Polanyian Meditations: In Search of a Post-Critical Logic* (Durham, NC: Duke University Press, 1985), 252-253.

[30] Ibid.

[31] Robert Doede, "The Decline of Anthropomorphic Explanation: From Animism to Deconstructionism," an unpublished paper delivered to the Regent College Faculty (1992).

[32] Ong, *Interfaces of the Word*, 125.

[33] Ibid., 129–130.

[34] Lonergan cited in Ong, *Interfaces of the Word*, 122.

[35] William H. Poteat, "Persons and Place: Paradigms in Communication," in *The Primacy of Persons and the Language of Culture: Essays by William H.*

Poteat, edited by James M. Nickell and James W. Stines (Columbia, MO: University of Missouri Press, 1993), 34.

[36] Ibid., 26.

[37] Kierkegaard, *Concluding Unscientific Postscript*, 173.

[38] Walter J. Ong, "Ramist Method and the Commercial Mind," in *Rhetoric, Romance, and Technology* (Ithaca, NY: Cornell University Press, 1971), 167 [my emphasis].

[39] Ibid., 180.

[40] Ibid., 186–187.

[41] Poteat, "Birth, Suicide, and the Doctrine of Creation," in *The Primacy of Persons*, 159.

[42] Romano Guardini, *The End of the Modern World: A Search for Orientation*, translated by Joseph Theman and Herbert Burke (Chicago: Henry Regnery Company, 1968), 99–100.

[43] Gabriel Marcel, *The Decline of Wisdom* (London: Harvill, 1954), 49.

[44] Poteat, *Polanyian Meditations*, 250.

[45] Søren Kierkegaard, *The Present Age & Of the Difference Between a Genius and an Apostle*, translated by Alexander Dru (New York: Harper & Row, 1962 [1846]), 33.

[46] Ellul, *The Humiliation of the Word*.

[47] Ibid., 33.

[48] C. John Sommerville, *The Secularization of Early Modern England: From Religious Culture to Religious Faith* (New York: Oxford University Press, 1992), 182.

[49] Steiner, *Real Presences*, 26–27.

[50] Aldous Huxley, *Brave New World Revisited* (New York: Harper & Row Publishers, 1958), 35–36.

[51] Søren Kierkegaard, *Søren Kierkegaard's Journals and Papers*, Volume 1 (A-E), translated and edited by Howard V. and Edna H. Hong (Bloomington, IN: Indiana University Press, 1967), 293.

[52] Ibid., 269.

[53] Steiner, *Language and Silence*, 53.

[54] Ibid.

[55] See Joseph Pieper, *Abuse of Language, Abuse of Power* (San Francisco: Ignatius Press, 1992), 30-31.

Chapter 3

[1] Peter Berger, *Pyramids of Sacrifice: Political Ethics and Social Change* (Garden City, NY: Anchor, 1976), 20.

[2] Walker Percy, *Lost in the Cosmos: The Last Self-Help Book* (New York: Farrar, Straus & Giroux, 1983), 1–2.

[3] Max Weber, *The Protestant Ethic and The Spirit of Capitalism*, translated by Talcott Parsons (Los Angeles: Roxbury, 1996), 82.

[4] Alister I. McFadyen, *The Call to Personhood: A Christian Theory of the Individual in Social Relationships* (Cambridge: Cambridge University Press, 1990), 122–123.

[5] Joseph Pieper, *Abuse of Language, Abuse of Power*, translated by Lothar Krauth (San Francisco: Ignatius Press, 1992), 7.

[6] Ibid., 10.

[7] Ibid., 21–22.

[8] Ibid., 26.

[9] Ibid., 28.

[10] Ibid., 29–30.

[11] Ibid., 20–21.

[12] Ibid., 34.

[13] James B. Twitchell, *Adcult USA: The Triumph of Advertising in American Culture* (New York: Columbia University Press, 1996), 18, 56.

[14] Ibid., 42.

[15] Ibid., 43.

[16] See Craig M. Gay, "Sensualists without Heart: Contemporary Consumerism in Light of the Modern Project," in *The Consuming Passion: Christianity & The Consumer Culture*, edited by Rodney Clapp (Downers Grove, IL: InterVarsity Press, 1998), 19–39.

[17] Dan Nimmo, *The Political Persuaders: The Techniques of Modern Election Campaigns* (Englewood Cliffs, NJ: Prentice Hall, 1970), 185.

[18] Ibid., 188.

[19] Ibid., 195.

[20] Michael Oakeshott, *Rationalism in Politics and Other Essays* (Indianapolis, IN: Liberty Fund, 1991), 9.

[21] See Glenn Tinder, *The Political Meaning of Christianity: The Prophetic Stance, An Introduction* (San Francisco: HarperSanFrancisco, 1989), 222–223.

²² Ibid., 222.

²³ Arnold Gehlen, *Man in the Age of Technology*, translated by Patricia Lipscomb (New York: Columbia University Press, 1980), 72.

²⁴ Oakeshott, *Rationalism in Politics*, 380.

²⁵ Alexis de Tocqueville, *Democracy in America*, translated by George Lawrence (Garden City, NY: Doubleday & Co./Anchor, 1969 [1848]).

²⁶ Ibid., 462.

²⁷ Ibid., 430.

²⁸ George Orwell, "Politics and the English Language," in *Inside the Whale and Other Essays* (London: Penguin, 1957), 153, 157.

²⁹ George Steiner, *Language and Silence: Essays on Language, Literature, and the Inhuman* (New Haven: Yale University Press, 1998 [1958]), 34–35.

³⁰ Pieper, *Abuse of Language*, 32–33, 34–35.

³¹ Marshall McLuhan, *Understanding Media: The Extensions of Man* (New York: Mentor, 1964), 88.

³² Jacques Ellul, *The Humiliation of the Word*, translated by Joyce Main Hanks (Grand Rapids, MI: Eerdmans, 1985), 162ff.

³³ Romano Guardini, *Letters From Lake Como: Explorations in Technology and the Human Race*, translated by Geoffrey W. Bromiley (Grand Rapids, MI: Eerdmans, 1994), 44–45.

³⁴ C. S. Lewis, *The Abolition of Man* (Glasgow: Collins, 1978 [1943]), 37.

³⁵ See John Macmurray, *The Boundaries of Science: A Study in the Philosophy of Psychology* (London: Faber & Faber, 1939), 163–164.

³⁶ Ibid., 164.

³⁷ Philosophical systems premised upon a kind of "ontology of violence" may be understood to reflect the intrinsic violence of the technological quest for mastery over nature. See, for example, John Milbank's discussion in *Theology and Social Theory: Beyond Secular Reason* (Oxford: Basil Blackwell, 1990), 278ff.

³⁸ Jean-François Lyotard, *The Postmodern Condition: A Report on Knowledge*, translated by Geoff Bennington and Brian Massumi, Theory and History of Literature, volume 10 (Minneapolis: University of Minnesota Press, 1984), xxiv.

³⁹ George Steiner, *Real Presences* (Chicago: University of Chicago Press, 1989), 119–120.

⁴⁰ Ibid., 132–133.

[41] Ibid., 92–93.

[42] Ibid.

[43] Friedrich Nietzsche, *The Will to Power*, edited by Walter Kaufmann, translated by Walter Kaufmann and R. J. Hollingdale (New York: Vintage Books, 1968), 451.

[44] Friedrich Nietzsche, *Beyond Good and Evil: Prelude to a Philosophy of the Future*, edited by Rolf Peter Horstmann and Judith Norman, translated by Judith Norman (Cambridge: Cambridge University Press, 2002), 123.

[45] Stephen M. Emmanuel, *Kierkegaard and the Concept of Revelation* (Albany: S.U.N.Y. Press, 1996), 16.

[46] Nietzsche, *The Anti-Christ*, translated by H. L. Mencken (Tuscon, AZ: See Sharp Press, 1999 [1888]), 91.

[47] Steiner, *Real Presences*, 86–87. Steiner writes: "I would define the claim to theory in the humanities as impatience systematized. Out of Judaism grown impatient at the everlasting delay of the messianic came strange fruit. Today, this impatience has taken on extreme, nihilistic urgency. It questions the very concepts of meaning and of form. It queries the possibility of any significant relations between word and world. It exalts the myths of theory above the facts of creation."

[48] Roger Lundin, *The Culture of Interpretation: Christian Faith and the Postmodern World* (Grand Rapids, MI: Eerdmans, 1993), 236.

[49] Pieper, *Abuse of Language*, 35–36.

[50] Ibid., 38–39.

Chapter 4

[1] Tinder, *Against Fate: An Essay on Personal Dignity* (Notre Dame, IN: University of Notre Dame Press, 1981), 9.

[2] William H. Poteat, *The Primacy of Persons and the Language of Culture: Essays by William H. Poteat*, edited by James M. Nickell and James W. Stines (Columbia, MO: University of Missouri Press, 1993), 91.

[3] Steiner, *Real Presences* (Chicago: University of Chicago Press, 1989), 3.

[4] Thorlief Boman, *Hebrew Thought Compared with Greek*, translated by Jules L. Moreau (New York: W. W. Norton, 1970), 67.

[5] Nelly Viallaneix, "Søren Kierkegaard: La Voix et L'Ouïe (A Propos des Quatre Discours Edifiants de 1843)," in *Les Etudes Philosophiques* (Janvier-Mars,1969): 211–224, unpublished translation by Paul Martens (1999).

[6] Boman, *Hebrew Thought*, 56.

[7] Ibid.

[8] Ibid.

[9] Ibid., 65–66.

[10] William H. Poteat, *Polanyian Meditations: In Search of a Post-Critical Logic* (Durham, NC: Duke University Press, 1985), 116.

[11] Ronald. L. Hall, *Word and Spirit: A Kierkegaardian Critique of the Modern Age* (Bloomington, IN: Indiana University Press, 1993), 31.

[12] Poteat, *Polanyian Meditations*, 129–130.

[13] Ibid., 128.

[14] Ibid.

[15] Ibid., 87–88.

[16] G. W. F. Hegel, *The Philosophy of History*, translated by J. Sibree (New York: Dover, 1956), 33.

[17] Martin Luther, *Luther's Works*, vol. 22: Sermons on the Gospel of John (St. Louis: Concordia Publishing House, 1957), 10.

[18] T. F. Torrance, *Theology in Reconstruction* (Eugene, OR: Wipf & Stock, 1996), 88.

[19] Kevin J. Vanhoozer, *Is There a Meaning in this Text? The Bible, the Reader, and the Morality of Literary Knowledge* (Grand Rapids, MI: Zondervan, 1998), 199.

[20] David K. Miell, "Barth on Persons in Relationship: A Case for Further Reflection?" in *Scottish Journal of Theology* 42 (1989): 541.

[21] Hall, *Word and Spirit*, 86.

[22] Ibid., 87.

[23] Steiner, *Real Presences*, 216.

[24] Nelly Viallaneix, *Kierkegaard: L'Unique Devant Dieu* (Paris: Les Editions du Cerf, 1974), unpublished translation by Paul Martens (1999).

[25] Hall, *Word and Spirit*, 74; or, as Kevin Vanhoozer put this in *Is There a Meaning in This Text?*: "Personhood is in large part a function of our dignity as communicative agents. From the viewpoint of Christian theology, persons are wholly determined neither by language (socio-linguistics) nor by genes (socio-biology). On the contrary, human persons are covenantal agents, whose stories, like that of Israel, depend in large measure on how they use their communicative freedom and assume their communicative responsibilities" (219).

[26] But just what is it that we are to listen to? In the first instance, it is God addressing us through what evangelical Protestants have long termed *the Word*, the Holy Scriptures. These texts are not to be understood simply as more-or-less faltering human attempts to express ineffable spiritual experiences; neither are they simply "interpretations" that call for endless reinterpretation and commentary. They are not to be understood to convey religious ideas that somehow intervene between the divine reality and our own, from which we may perhaps deduce truths about God. Rather the Holy Scriptures must be understood to be God's words addressed personally and directly to each one of us in and by the power of his Spirit. The Holy Scriptures are direct, personal, dialogical communication.

Of course, this raises difficult questions concerning the obviously human authorship of the texts as well as questions concerning their interpretation, questions that have generated a vast literature and that we cannot possibly answer satisfactorily here. Yet T. F. Torrance has helpfully suggested that the relationship between God's *Word* and the biblical texts might be said to be analogous to the relation between numbers and physical reality in natural science. Are numbers something that we *invent*? Torrance queries in *Theology in Reconstruction* (Eugene, OR: Wipf & Stock, 1996), or are they something that we *find* in nature? The answer is evidently—if mysteriously—*both*. While we do not actually find ready-made numerical equations in nature, we do find that natural processes are often exactly explicable in terms of the mathematical operations that we have formulated. Nature bespeaks a rational ordering to which our minds are evidently already mysteriously suited. Even as we herald the individual genius of the likes of Descartes, Newton, or Einstein, then, we recognize their individual discoveries to be implacably *objective* and not simply individually and/or socially constructed. No one has yet been able to say just how and why this remarkable consonance is possible. Perhaps it is not possible to do so. So it is also, Torrance argues, with the *Word of God* in biblical theology. The Word is obviously expressed in and through human words, and yet it is not thereby prevented from confronting us, at least if we have "ears to hear," as a direct Divine *address*. How is this possible? Again, it may not be possible for us to say. As Torrance comments: "No work of ours can establish a bridge between our understanding and the Truth of God. Knowledge of God is in accordance with his nature as Spirit, and takes its rise from his living personal action upon us. The relation between our statements about God and God himself in his own Truth is not one that we can create or describe in statements, but one that we can only allow to happen to us and which we accept in yielding our minds and speech obediently and gratefully to his revealing and saving acts" (93).

The modern assumptions that the biblical texts are simply more-or-less valuable records of past spiritual experiences, then, or that they are the product of religious "genius"—assumptions dating back to late-eighteenth century Romanticism—while not perhaps intellectually refutable, betray a decision to stand *over* the texts and to *use* them, often for extra-biblical purposes. Such assumptions obviate the need to *listen* to the texts, and it is not particularly surprising that those who labor under them often find themselves *deaf* to *the Word* speaking through the texts. The extraordinary growth of the Christian church throughout the modern world gives evidence of the astonishing fact that *Yahweh's "dabhar"* continues to be *heard* by those remaining open to the possibility of *hearing* God's *voice* in the Holy Scriptures. We ought, then, as was said of the boy Samuel, to take care to let none of God's words "fall to the ground" (1 Sam 3:19).

[27] Viallaneix, "Søren Kierkegaard: La Voix et L'Ouïe."

[28] Viallaneix, *L'Unique Devant Dieu.*

[29] Ibid.

[30] Hall, *Word and Spirit,* 55.

[31] Poteat, *The Primacy of Persons,* 262.

[32] Søren Kierkegaard, *For Self-Examination/Judge for Yourself,* translated by Howard V. and Edna H. Hong (Princeton, NJ: Princeton University Press, 1990 [1848]), 47-48.